LOST HISTORY
of
America

LOST HISTORY
of
America

JODY D. KIMBRELL

Lost History of America

Copyright © 2021 by Jody D. Kimbrell. All rights reserved.

No part of this publication may be reproduced, stored in a retrieval system or transmitted in any way by any means, electronic, mechanical, photocopy, recording or otherwise without the prior permission of the author except as provided by USA copyright law.

The opinions expressed by the author are not necessarily those of URLink Print and Media.

1603 Capitol Ave., Suite 310 Cheyenne, Wyoming USA 82001
1-888-980-6523 | admin@urlinkpublishing.com

URLink Print and Media is committed to excellence in the publishing industry.

Book design copyright © 2021 by URLink Print and Media. All rights reserved.

Published in the United States of America

Library of Congress Control Number: 2020913611
ISBN 978-1-64753-443-1 (Paperback)
ISBN 978-1-64753-444-8 (Digital)

20.10.20

DEDICATION

This book is dedicated to my family: my children, Gerry, Jason, and Candy, who had to put up with Mom spouting off history at them *all the time*; my mom, Anna, who spreads all my history stories; and my husband, Mike, who put up with old books everywhere in our home, which were in various states of repair, and built my bookcases so I could house my babies. He also reminded me who had inspired me to share Lost History with the world, so a special dedication goes to President Donald Trump: your constant vigilance, refusal to submit to pressure to abandon the American people, and your steadfast, stubborn actions to stay the course to beat terrorism reminded me of our ancestors who faced down an empire—dedicated in their mission to protect Liberty too.

My special thanks I offer to the Heavenly Father, who introduced me to the Founders and the everyday people who gave America her freedom.

Contents

Preface 9
Introductory Remarks 11
Causes Of The American Revolution And Events That
    Led To The Birth Of The United States Of America ...13
Campaign Of 1776 40
Actual Events At The Famous Crossing Of The Delaware ...58
A Traitors Story 81
Gloom And Doom-1781 84
Providence Embraces Liberty
    1782 To 1784 87
Liberty Won, Birth Of A Nation-1784 To 1788 91
Founding Facts 95
Some Interesting Facts And Word Meanings 101
Reflections 104
History Test-Guess The Year 107
Bibliography 109
Endnotes 111

PREFACE

When we read current history books, we assume they are correct and complete. Those lines, describing the events and text of our past, are what we pass on, and if they are incomplete then history is lost. Those happenings become what the reader or the writer of the history reports, and the actual events are changed forever. I discovered this when attending a farm auction in Central Illinois. I purchased an 1880 volume of the History of Peoria County. It was abused, spineless, and had loose covers, but it was packed with information about the founding of Peoria County. I was so excited to have found it. After rebinding, with a new spine and label, I read a detailed, fact-filled history of my home.

After finishing it I called our local library and asked if they had this volume, they did, so I took my volume and went to view theirs. My book is over six inches thick and is jam-packed with information about people, happenings, and engravings. The librarian laid her copy next to mine. It was less than two inches thick and had none of the histories, mine had! The title and the author were the same, but the book had been revised, and the people who built Peoria County had been eliminated!

I was shocked and compelled from that point forward to gather history as it was written at the time. I soon learned that Providence was at work. His plan to give Back America's history had me gathering books, and what I found would make you cry. Books, written and read by our Founders, ancestors, and people who walked this earth when America was born were abused, burned, ripped, and filthy. The books' covers and spines were torn off and in total, unwanted condition. They held the *Lost History of America* I was searching for.

Armed with deerskin, glue, and leather cleaner/conditioner, I learned how to save books, thus saving America's history. You, the reader, will be joining George Washington as he grows to manhood and starts his journey to the birth of our beloved country. You will stand next to him on the battlefield, feeling his anxious concerns and reveling in his triumphs. You will meet the everyday people who rose up and fought for liberty and the freedom you enjoy today. Their books, their language, and their determination will embrace you as you read the events that led to a free America, and your heart will swell with love for the greatest country ever created by the Hand of God.

INTRODUCTORY REMARKS

In entering upon any pursuit, it is well to place distinctly in view the objects we propose to accomplish. History is the school of politics. It opens the hidden springs of human affairs. It sets before us striking instances of virtue, enterprise, courage, generosity, patriotism, and by a natural principle of emulation, incites us to copy such noble examples. It leads to the rise, grandeur, revolutions, and fall of empires and points out the influence the manners of a people exert upon a government, as well as the influence the government exerts upon the manners of a people. It illustrates the blessings of political union, the miseries of faction, the dangers of *unbridled* liberty, and the abuses by despotic power. It displays the dealings of God with mankind, calls upon us to regard, with awe, His darker judgments, and again it awakens the liveliest of emotions of gratitude for His benevolence, cultivates a sense of dependence on Him, and impresses us with a conviction of His justice.

History furnishes matter for conversation, chastens the imagination, enlarges the range of thought, and strengthens and disciplines the mind. History is what guides the future. What happens if history is lost? Supreme Court justices become ignorant, using fragments of history to render decisions upon the population. Some even impose their own ideology, which likens to *putting false words into the mouths of our Founders*. The false words become fact, and the population lives with the results. Groups form to impose their beliefs, and as more history is replaced, more false information is spread. Therefore the truth and our past slowly die with the ages.

This book corrects what has been lost and gives the true and uncorrupted history of America. Even those whose ideologies will be bashed by these words cannot deny this book, as its words were written when our Founders walked this earth.

The words of *Lost History of America* will ring out and the tree of Liberty and Truth will spread its branches, overshadowing those who will be in shock when they read the words of our Founders. And amid all the flare-up of political strife, by which some will be agitated, let us ever bear aloft the Motto:

The Union: One Inseparable

"How long wilt thou go about oh thou backsliding daughter? For the Lord has created a new thing on the earth; a woman shall compass the man" (Jeremiah 31:22, KJV).

Her name is the United States of America, born from the heart of God.

jerUSAlem

CAUSES OF THE AMERICAN REVOLUTION AND EVENTS THAT LED TO THE BIRTH OF THE UNITED STATES OF AMERICA

Act of Oppression upon The Land of Liberty—1748 to 1774

I have chosen to start with this time period because of its importance to the present time. There have been laws written, policy put forth, and claims as to *what* our Founders actually intended this country should be. Much of this rhetoric was written by individuals whose interpretations, in my opinion, implemented their ideologies while claiming they were *following* the Constitution and the thoughts and wishes of the Founders. Let me tell you, a lot of their interpretation is bunk. Here is the sequence of events that led to a free United States of America.

The French/English Indian Wars—1748

(*That is right, folks, the colonists and the natives were thrust into wars because France and England could not get along.*)

In 1748, after many long years of strife, then a period of peace, then strife renewed, those two nations finally agreed to peace. They believed themselves the arbitrators of mankind, the pacifiers of the world, and supposed they were establishing the colonial system on a basis that would endure for ages. They signed the treaty of Aix-la-Chapelle, which restored tranquillity to America.[1]

At this time the woods of Virginia sheltered the youthful George Washington. Born beneath the roof of a Westmoreland farmer, almost from infancy, his lot was the lot of an orphan. No academy had welcomed him; no college crowned him in honors; to read, to write, to cipher—these had been his degrees in knowledge. And now at sixteen years of age, in quest of an honest living, encountering incredible toil, wandering the backwoods and the banks of the Shenandoah among the skin-clad natives with their scalps and rattles—holding a bearskin a splendid couch—this stripling surveyor, with no companion but his unlettered associates, no implements of science but his compass and chain, contrasted strongly with the imperial magnificence of the congress of Aix-la-Chapelle.[2]

Yet God chose not these monarchs and learned men but a Virginia stripling to give an impulse to human affairs, and as far as events can depend on an individual, had placed the rights and destinies of countless millions in the keeping of a widow's son. The voice of that boy was soon to be heard in the din of battle, and the mind of what we would call a blue-collar worker, strengthened and matured by years of hard work, was to guide the steps of his suffering country through a long and bloody war, and finally lay the foundation of the noblest structure of human freedom ever designed by man.

The colonists and natives had but a short time to reap the benefits of peace. With the conclusion of the treaty, their prospects were again clouded, and the sound of approaching war filled the land with anxiety and gloom. After an interval of about eight years (1748-1756), Great Britain formally declared war against France. The cause was borders-alleged encroachments of the French on the frontiers of the colonies in America belonging to the English crown.

French possessions reached from the mouth of the St. Lawrence to Montreal. The French erected houses on Lake Ontario, planted New Orleans, discovered the Mississippi, and claimed the vast tract watered by it and its tributary streams. They were determined to connect their north and south possessions. While they were in the prosecution of this design, a company of traders from London and

Virginia had obtained a grant from the king of six hundred thousand acres on and near Ohio and erected fur houses for trade with the natives. The Canadian governor feared these traders would prevent the French design, seized some of the traders, and imprisoned them in Canada.

Lt. Governor Robert Dinwiddie of Virginia demanded the reason of this hostile conduct. This message was entrusted to George Washington, who began the line of service which would lead to the independence of his country.

On October 31, 1753, Washington left Williamsburg, Virginia, traveled through the forests and mountains, lost his horse, and continued the trek of about 560 miles on foot. On December 13, he reached the French fort and delivered the letter to the commander.

Washington returned to Williamsburg with the answer. The commander's reply was he had taken possession of the country under the direction of the governor-general of Canada, whose order should be obeyed. This was not satisfactory, and the Virginians were instructed to resist encroachments by force of arms. Troops were raised in Virginia and joined by an independent company from South Carolina, totaling about four hundred. The command of the expedition was given to Washington who, in April 1754, marched into the territory in dispute. Meeting at Great Meadows, he attacked and defeated the French force and erected Fort Necessity.

Receiving reinforcements from New York and Carolina, he proceeded toward Fort Du Queene, erected on the fork of the Alleghany and Monongahela rivers.

Hearing that De Villiers was approaching from this fort, Washington retired to Fort Necessity to await reinforcements. De Villiers attacked with 1,500 troops and, after a vicious attack, offered Washington honorable terms of capitulation. He accepted and returned with his troops to Virginia.[3]

In the same year delegates from the seven colonies assembled at Albany to form a treaty of friendship with the Six Nations, negotiated with the Oneida, a member tribe of the Iroquois called the People of the Standing Stone. Most of the Iroquois sided with England, but the Oneida chose America's side. After accomplishing this business, they proceeded to adopt a plan of union, similar in its construction to the present Constitution, to be submitted to the colonial legislatures and to parliament for their approval. The plan was rejected by parliament because they considered it gave too much power to the people and rejected by the colonies because it gave too much power to the king.

England was already jealous of the colonial assemblies and saw in them a spirit that, unless checked in this infantile state, might soon become too powerful to control.

Since the colonies failed in their plan of union, they joined England in the war with France over borders and encroachments. In the spring of 1754, General Edward Braddock arrived with a large force of English troops and was given the authority as commander-in-chief over the English and American Colonial Forces. His campaign would be against Fort du Queene, with a second against Niagara under Governor William Shirley and a third against Crown Point under General John Johnson. While these preparations were going on, another plan for attacking the French in Nova Scotia was carried out. Commander Generals Robert Monckton and John Winslow and three thousand troops sailed from Boston. The resistance was slight and in short time the English gained possession of the whole province, with the loss of only three men.

Braddock was a brave man possessed of great military skill, but educated in the science of war as then taught in Europe, he knew little of Indian warfare. His severe strictness in camp approached arrogance, and unfortunately for him, he entertained supreme contempt for the colonial troops and the advice of the American officers. When Washington, who was his aid-de-camp, suggested the propriety of employing the Indians as scouts and advance parties, he disdained the advice, which, if followed, would have saved his army and changed a shameful defeat into a glorious victory.

Taking none of the precautions, on July 9, a few miles from the fort, he fell into an ambush of the French and Indians. The English troops broke rank when they heard the war whoop of the Indians and would have fled, except Braddock rallied to preserve a regular order of battle, keeping them cooped up like sheep—fair marks for the unseen enemy.

The slaughter was dreadful, and every officer on horseback, except Washington, was shot down; he, riding over every part of the field, had two horses shot from under him and four balls lodged in his coat. The Indians afterward asserted they had repeatedly fired at him with rifles that had never missed the mark before; at Length they were convinced the Great Spirit shielded him. God had preserved his life to be a leader in the great struggle of his country for liberty.[4]

This war carried on, not reaching a peace treaty till 1763 when France ceded to Great Britain all her Northern settlements in America. The bloody war, which had so long raged on the American frontiers, was at Length closed, and the provincial soldiers returned to their homes to enjoy a short respite of peace before they again took the field, this time in the struggle for liberty against the tyranny of England. Soon the causes of specific events would unfold and lead to the most interesting happenings of any in the history of the time. This overthrow of tyranny and despotism in the United Colonies would erect an altar of human freedom sacred to liberty unlike any the world had ever seen.

A dark cloud had hung over the nations of the Old World for more than a thousand years. The rulers were the rich and the great, and they swayed the rod of empire with no gentle hand. The groans of the oppressed arose faintly through the gloom that surrounded them, yet they entered the ear of the Most High, and He, in His own good time, formed a plan for civil and religious emancipation of the world.

A new era was to commence in the West. The link, which for ages had bound England to America by the corroding influence of evil ministers, was to be broken; a new government was to be formed—one based on justice for all and in which the lowest voice as well as the highest could be heard. The causes of the American Revolution, which ended in the firm establishment of our liberties, lay in the jealousy, tyranny, and oppression of the English government. The American colonists had freely given their blood and treasure for the maintenance of the power of the British crown. They had rushed to the battlefield, endured every hardship, and patiently submitted to the wrongs from the very hand they had strengthened. They had regarded England with reverence and affection and never dreamed of leaving the paternal roof, until the unholy chastisement of a parent's hand alienated their love, expelled them from the threshold, and compelled them to seek shelter and security behind the bulwarks of righteous insurrection.

In the early period of their colonial existence, Great Britain had troubled them but little about their internal policy, being satisfied with a monopoly of their trade and aid in the war with France. The colonies had increased in strength and population, and the war ended in a vast amount of territory for the English crown. This should have dictated a relaxation of their authority; instead they rose in their demands and increased the restraints. Heavy taxes were imposed to pay off England's national debt, and it was forgotten the Americans were descended from the same forefathers as themselves and heirs to the same rights. Also bearing their share in the expense of the war, the colonies made no objections, but they did object to the system of taxation in which they had no right to be heard—something current American government officials should pay heed to.

In 1765, Lord George Grenville, after giving notice to the American agents in London, introduced into parliament a long-cherished scheme for the purpose of raising revenue from the American colonies by means of a stamp duty. Petitions opposing the tax poured in from the Americans, and at first it met with opposition in the House of Commons. The following text took place in the halls of Parliament as those who chose to oppress America argued with those who wanted equality for the colonies.[5]

Charles Townsend, at the close of a speech supporting the act, asked, "And those Americans, children planted by our care, nourished by our indulgence and protected by our arms until they have grown up to a degree of strength and opulence, will they grudge to contribute their mite to relieve us from the heavy load of national expense which we lie under?"

Col. Isaac Barre exclaimed, "Planted by our care!... No!... Our oppression planted them in America. They fled our tyranny into an uncultivated land... They are nourished by our indulgence!... No!... They grew by our neglect... They protected by our arms! No!... They have taken up arms in our defense, exerted their valor amid their constant and laborious industry for the defense of a country, which, while its frontiers were drenched in blood... The people were loyal but would vindicate their liberties if they should be violated."

But the eloquence of Col. Barre and the remonstrance of the colonies could not change the avaricious feelings of the parliament and the bill passed by large majority. The mistake of shortsighted legislators and poor readers of human nature did not see that in the passage of an act so odious to the colonies they had accelerated the cause of liberty. They were the first to *awaken the sleeping giant*. Dr. Benjamin Franklin wrote to Mr. Charles Thompson, "The sun of liberty is set; you must light the candles of industry and economy." To which he answered, "I was apprehensive that other lights would be the consequences, and I foresee the opposition that will be made."[6]

By this act no written instrument could be legal unless stamped paper was used, which had to be purchased at an exorbitant price from the British agents. For a breach of this law, the colonists would be tried without jury before any marine court. The passage of this law was received with sorrow and dismay. Parliament had turned a deaf ear and showed by the passage of the act a determination to treat them, not as English citizens, but as lowly servants of the crown. They must either surrender without a struggle their liberty; or oppose strongly and firmly the avarice of a nation, the most powerful in the world and to which they had been accustomed to turn their eyes in fond affection as their Motherland.

The colonies wasted no time in making their decision and proclaiming it to the world. The Virginian legislature was in session when the news arrived. Patrick Henry, a brilliant young man, opposed it with all the strength of a great mind. He brought before the house five resolutions, which were adopted and which closed by declaring "That any individual, who, by speaking or acting, assert that any class of men except the general assembly of the province, had a right to impose taxation, he should be considered an enemy of the colony."[7]

In advocating these resolutions, he boldly denounced the policy of the British government and declared the king had acted the part of a tyrant. Growing warm with his subject and alluding to the fate of other tyrants, he exclaimed, "Caesar had his Brutus, Charles I his Cromwell and George III..."

Pause while the room erupts in stunned response.

"Treason! Treason!" arose from every part of the house as the members realized the consequences of the words.

Pausing till the tumult had ended, Henry added, "... George III may profit by their example. If this is treason, make the most of it."[8]

Similar sentiments flew like lightning through the other colonies. The tongues and pens of the citizens labored in kindling the latent sparks of patriotism. The press called upon the citizens to resist it. Before the proceedings in Virginia had become known in Massachusetts, her legislature passed a resolution in favor of a continental congress, fixed a day in October for its meeting in New York, and sent letters to the speakers of the other colonial legislatures requesting their concurrence.

On the first Tuesday in October, delegates from all the colonies, excepting Virginia, North Carolina, Georgia, and New Hampshire, assembled in New York and agreed upon a declaration of rights. asserting, in strong language, their exemption from all taxes not imposed by their representatives and their right of trial by jury and drew up a petition to the king with memos to both houses of parliament. It was signed by all of the delegates, except Tom Ruggles of New York and Mr. Robert Ogden of New Jersey.

On the arrival of the first of November, the day the obnoxious Stamp Act was to go into effect, hardly a sheet of the stamped paper, which had been sent to America, could be found. It had been destroyed or re-shipped to England, used as wrapping paper. The general aversion to the act was demonstrated in a variety of ways. Boston, on that first morning in November, which ushered the Stamp Act into existence, welcomed the destroying agency in the mournful accents of a funeral knell. Shops were closed and effigies of unpopular characters were paraded through the streets and burned.

In Portsmouth, New Hampshire, the day was started with strong evidence of hostility and grief. Notice having been given to the friends of Liberty to attend her funeral, a coffin inscribed with the word *Liberty* was borne along in solemn procession to the grave. The muffled drums, the death march, the booming minute guns, and the tolling hells as they threw out their mournful tones upon the air, gave evidences of the greatness of their bereavement. On their arrival at the place of internment, a eulogy was pronounced upon the deceased. Scarcely was it ended before the coffin was taken up, the inscription was changed to *Liberty Revived*, the bells rang out in joyous peals, and satisfaction beamed on the faces of the people as Liberty was given life again.

In New York, the act was printed under the title of "*The Folly of England and the Ruin of America*," and distributed through the streets."[9]

In different parts of the country, stamp masters were compelled to resign their offices to prevent being mobbed. The Stamp Act was so formed that the penalty of disobedience would be no less than the suspension of the whole machinery of the political and social order and the creation of the state of anarchy.

No trade or navigation, no process against an offender, no apprentice could be indentured, no marriage, no estate settled, not even a diploma presented unless the stamp duty was paid. By degree, however, things began to assume their normal course and all kinds of business were transacted in open defiance of the act.

Associations under the title of the Sons of Liberty were formed in every part of the country. They denounced the Stamp Act and resolved to defend those who fell into the hands of British tyranny because of their clinging to their rights as freemen. Merchants would not import goods and families denied themselves the use of foreign luxuries. Two members who produced a steady stream of news and opinion were Benjamin Edes, journalist, and John Gill of the *Boston Gazette*. Within a very short time, over two thousand men had been organized under Ebenezer McIntosh, a Boston shoemaker.[10]

The information about the violence in the colonies was received in England with consternation and alarm. It was well Lord Grenville was dismissed and the Marquis of Rockingham, a friend of America, appointed in his place. He, with many others, felt that the Stamp Act could only be enforced at the point of a bayonet and that it must be repealed or the death knell of their power would be tolled in America.

A proposition for its repeal was accordingly laid before parliament. Lord Grenville strongly opposed and declared that to repeal the act would disgrace the government and encourage rebellion. He demanded to know when America was emancipated and by what reason they claimed exemption in defraying expenses incurred in protecting them.

Mr. William Pitt arose to reply. In his speech he said:

> We are told America is obstinate—America is in open rebellion. Sir, I rejoice that America has resisted. Three million people so dead to all the feelings of liberty as voluntarily to submit to be slaves, would have been fit instruments to make slaves of all the rest. When were the colonies emancipated?... When were they made slaves?... I speak from accurate knowledge when I say the profit of Great Britain from the trade of the colonies is two million per year. This is the field that carried you triumphantly through the war. This is what America sends you for protection; and shall a miserable pensioner come with a boast that he can fetch peppercorns at the loss of millions to a nation. I know the valor of your troops—the skill of your officers—the force of this country—but in such a cause, your success would be hazardous. America, if she fell, would fall like a strong man; she would embrace the pillars of the state and pull down the constitution with her. Is this your boasted peace, not to sheathe the sword in the scabbard, but in the bowels of your countrymen? The Americans have been wronged; they have been driven by injustice! Will you punish them for the madness you have caused? No, let this country be the first to resume its prudence and temper; I will pledge myself for the colonies that on their part animosity and resentment will cease. My opinion, repeal the Stamp Act—absolutely—totally and immediately.[11]

The repeal passed the House of Commons but met violent opposition in the House of Lords. Lord Camden, advocating for the colonies, said, "*Taxation & Representation are inseparable.* It is external. law, for whatever is a man own is his own, and no man has a right to take it from him without consent. Whoever does commits a robbery."[12]

The bill of repeal, after a stormy debate, finally passed but was accompanied by a declaratory act, which declared that parliament had a right to bind the colonies in all cases whatever. (Reminds me of the Democrats so-called "Fairness Act" where they get to say who I listen to on the radio.)

The news of the repeal was received with expressions of joy. All England joined in the applause. In America there was public thanksgiving, goods were imported, and a general calm succeeded the storm that had raged so violently.

But among the people of New England and New York, less joy and gratitude were displayed and felt. They feared, from the passage of the declaratory act, this was only a truce in the war against American rights. In the mirror of the past they saw the future reflected, and trembled at the picture.

The result showed their suspicions were just. A change in the ministry took place in July, in which the Marquis of Rockingham was removed and a new cabinet formed under the direction of Mr. Pitt, afterward Earl of Chatham.

On June 17, during the confinement of Mr. Pitt in the country by sickness, Charles Townsend, chancellor of the exchequer, brought before parliament another plan for taxing America—by imposing duties on all tea, glass, and painter's colors that should be imported in to the colonies. The bill was passed by both houses with little opposition and followed by another bill, the Act of Trade and Navigation, which was to be enforced by appointing officers of the Navy as customhouse officers. Previous to this new act of tyranny, the legislative power of New York had been suspended until it should furnish the king's troops with certain supplies at the expense of the colony.

Early in 1768 the general court of Massachusetts sent a petition to the king and addressed circular letters to the colonial assemblies, asking for their co-operation in obtaining the redress of their grievances. The ministry was alarmed and demanded of the court that they should rescind the vote directing circulars to be sent. The assembly refused and the governor dissolved them. This attempt to intimidate did nothing but strengthen the opposition.

Shortly after this the customhouse officers, for violating some of the new commercial regulations, seized a sloop belonging to John Hancock. The people attacked the houses of the officers and they were compelled to leave town. The refractory spirit of the citizens of Boston had been displayed on many occasions. General Gage was ordered to station a regiment of soldiers in the city to overawe the citizens. Their appearance only served to excite the indignation of the inhabitants. Soldiers paraded the streets, the roar of artillery broke in upon the quiet of their Sabbath, and their wives were exposed to insult from the soldiery as they attended church.[13]

Early the following year the governor of Massachusetts was directed to report citizen conducts and to make strict inquiries as to all treasons committed and to send the offenders to England for trial. The legislature immediately passed resolutions denying the right of the king to remove any citizen out of the colony. He dismissed the assembly.

They met in private homes and entered into a written agreement not to import any taxed articles from England.

The inhabitants of Charlestown broke off all commerce with Rhode Island and Georgia, who they charged with having acted a most infamous part from the beginning of the present glorious struggle for the preservation of American rights. This had its effect and Georgia signed a non-importation agreement on September 19, Providence on October 10, and Rhode Island on October 30. All had signed the agreement except Portsmouth, New Hampshire, where Governor John Wentworth had address enough to prevent it and keep it quiet. There were few schools in the county and the bulk of the people were very illiterate.[14]

Boston and New York entered into the non-importation agreement as early as August the preceding year. Before the present year was out, they began to be embarrassed. The British officers either by their own thought or through hints from home offered merchants the liberty of having their goods directed to them as if intended for the army, and many got in, especially in New York. Several imported into Boston and sold freely. This occasioned alarm and the people assembled at Faneuil Hall to report the businesses rendering the non-importation agreement abortive.

Mr. Theophilus Lillie, observing the gross partiality to certain merchants who received British goods, ignored the non-importation agreement and allowed them to sell, while other merchants were exposed for breaking the agreement, His was pointed out as a shop that was to be shunned; a piece of paper identifying his shame was placed above his door.

Mr. Richardson attempted to remove it and was driven indoors by a number of boys throwing stones at him and his house. Provoked instead of endangered by the assault, he drew his pistol, fired, and killed Christopher Snider, a lad of eleven who was recorded in the public prints as the first martyr to the noble cause of liberty.[15]

(History note: The "shot heard around the world" story comes from a poem written in 1886 called "The Minute Man.")

The death of a child is what brought the blood of the Bostonians to a boil.[16]

On the second of March, an affray took place between some regular troops and some rope makers, in which the soldiers were beaten. Angry feelings were aroused, and on the evening of the fifth a crowd of citizens attacked the city guards under Captain Thomas Preston, pelting them with stones and snowballs until the word to fire was given. Three citizens were killed and several wounded. The alarm spread everywhere, the bells were rung, drums were heard, and the cry to arms was raised. The troops were removed from the city, with Preston and his men tried for murder. All were acquitted except two who were convicted of manslaughter. The dead included Crispus Attucks—a free black man who led the crowd—Samuel Grey, Samuel

Maverick, James Caldwell, and Patrick Carr, who died ten days later. This day is known as the Boston Massacre.[17]

The very same day, Lord Fredrick North introduced a bill to parliament which passed, removing all the duties laid excepting on tea. But still, declaring the right to tax the colonies remained. No tea had been imported and the commercial part of Britain was feeling the effect. The naked question of principle on taxation was thus presented. It had been an insidious plan, but the energy of the Americans had foiled it completely. Threepence a pound was nothing, but the principle of tyranny was strong and the resistance was as unyielding as though it had been an act of confiscation. Tea was shipped in vast quantities, but the people refused it; Charleston would not permit it to be sold, storing it in wet basements till it was ruined.

In Boston, a large crowd descended onto Griffin's wharf at the same instant a group of men dressed as Indians ran among the laden ships of tea. In about two hours, they had hoisted out and broke open 342 chests of tea and dumped them into the harbor. They were unnoticed as the multitude of spectator's served as a covering party to the scene. No damage was done to the vessels, and when they were finished all returned quietly to their own towns and homes. This day is known as the Boston Tea Party.[18]

Parliament, in order to punish the Bostonians, passed the Boston Port Bill, which prevented landing and shipping of goods. The customhouse was moved to Salem, which refused to raise its fortunes on the ruin of their countrymen. Marblehead, a town north of Boston, generously offered them the use of their warehouses and harbor.

The following March, two other tyrannical bills were passed in parliament. One subverted the whole constitution and charter of Massachusetts, taking all power out of the hands of the people and vesting it in the crown. The other authorized the governor to send to England or to some other colony any person accused of murder or other capital offense committed in aiding magistrates in the discharge of their duty.

Shortly after, General Thomas Gage arrived in supersede Governor Thomas Hutchinson as governor and to enforce the odious Port Bill of 1774. The assembly resolved, "*The injustice, inhumanity and cruelty of the act exceed all our powers of expression and declared they would leave it to the just censure of others, and appeal to the God of the world.*"[19]

The legislature of Virginia appointed June 1—the day the act was to go into effect—as a day of fasting, humiliation, and prayer to implore God to give them *one heart* and *one mind* firmly to oppose by all just and proper means every injury to American rights. Governor John Murray Dunmore resented this proceeding and dissolved the assembly. They', however, formed an association, resolved not to use any imports until the act was repealed, and concluded by proposing a General Congress of the colonies.

On the fourth of September, the proposed congress, consisting of deputies from eleven colonies assembled in Philadelphia, passed a resolution highly commending the conduct of Massachusetts in the conflict with the wicked ministers and exhorted all to press on in the cause of liberty. They drew up a Bill of Rights, entered into an agreement for themselves and for their constituents to cease all importations from Great Britain, and adopted measures for organizing committees in every town and city; to see that this agreement was enforced by every species of popular influence.

They addressed a letter to General Gage, entreating him to desist from military operations. They also voted an address to the king: one to Great Britain and another to Canada. Their petition to the king entreated him to restore to them their violated rights—their rights as English freemen. In their address to English people, they declared "*That they never would be hewers of wood and drawers of water, for any ministry or nation in the world.*"[20]

This frank expression of feeling on the part of the colonists aroused the indignation of the British government. America, they said, had long wished to be independent, and to prevent this was the duty of every Englishman, and that it must be done at every hazard.

Boston Neck was fortified—powder and other military brought in by Gage. The assembly met in Salem and appointed a committee of safety and supplies then sent messengers to New Hampshire, Rhode Island, and Connecticut to raise an army of twenty thousand men.

England could see the upheaval of violence from colonial indignation, refused to listen to the warning sound and determined upon another act of oppression.

The line in the sand had been drawn.

War—1775 to 1783

Matters were now rapidly approaching a crisis, the spirit of resentment was being fanned into flame, a dark and bloody cloud was hovering over the land, and the great question was soon to be decided—whether they should be servants or freemen; whether their names should be blackened with stigma of rebellion or handed down to posterity as the saviors of their country.

On the tenth of February, a bill was passed restricting the commerce of the New England states and forbidding them to fish on the banks of Newfoundland (north Canadian town). The same restrictions soon after extended to all of the colonies. The people of Massachusetts were pronounced rebels, and ten thousand men with several ships of the line (naval warships of heavy construction; two columns of opposing warships would maneuver to bring the greatest weight of broadside guns to bear) were ordered to America to enforce obedience.[21]

The committee of safety and supplies had collected a large quantity of stores and ammunition at Concord, about twenty miles from Boston. General Thomas Gage, deeming it advisable to possession of them, sent out a detachment of eight hundred men under the command of Colonel Francis Smith and Major John Pitcairn.

Notwithstanding the precaution of the British officers to prevent the spread of intelligence, the march of the troops had been made known by expresses and signal guns.

On their arrival at Lexington, five miles from Concord, they saw the militia of the place was drawn up to receive them. The regulars approached within musket-shot when Major Pitcairn, riding forward with drawn sword, exclaimed, "Disperse you rebels! Throw down your arms and disperse."[22]

Not being obeyed he discharged his pistol and ordered his soldier to fire. They fired and killed eight men and wounded several others. The rest dispersed, but firing continued. The enemy then proceed to Concord and destroyed the greater part of the stores.

The militia had in the meantime assembled, and a skirmish ensued in which a number were killed. The British commenced their retreat but were pressed on all sides by the now-enraged Americans.[23]

The whole country was in arms. Every wall, house and tree contributed to shelter some exasperated New Englander. A perpetual fire was kept up in this manner during the whole length of their weary and laborious march until, at night, with a loss of 273 men, they encamped on Bunker Hill, under the protection of the men of war, and the next day passed over to Boston.

The intelligence of these events spread like wildfire through the land. The torch of war had been lit, and blood had been offered on the altar of liberty: fearfully was the death of those patriots slain at Lexington and Concord to be avenged. Couriers galloped in every direction, beating a drum and shouting in tones that thrilled every ear that heard,

"To arms, to arms! Liberty or death!"[24]

The streets of Lexington and Concord had been soaked in blood and the country was in ablaze.

General Israel Putnam heard it. Leaving his oxen in the field, he stayed not to change his farmer's dress but, springing on his swiftest horse, was soon seen speeding along the road to Boston. Those who saw that rough form fly past knew that wild work would be done. Old age, with hands trembling from palsy, threw aside the cushioned crutch and grasped the deadly firelock. Mechanics left their shops and farmers the plough, and bursting away from their wives and children sped onto the field of battle where liberty was to be bought with blood.[25]

In a few days, a line of encampment stretched from Roxbury to the river. An army of twenty thousand men environed Mystic and the British forces in Boston. In New Haven, hearing the news, Benedict

Arnold, a druggist, gathered around him a band of volunteers and marched onto the scene of strife. At Boston, he formed the bold plan of seizing the important fortresses of Ticonderoga and Crown Point.

Having received instructions from the committee of safety to raise a sufficient number of men for the purpose, he marched on Bennington where he found Capt. Ethan Allen had collected a large band of 230 Green Mountain Boys, so-called from their residing within the limits of the Green Mountains—a brave, hardy generation and chiefly settlers from New Hampshire, Massachusetts, and Connecticut (now called Vermont)—separate colonies but united as one. They marched on a side by side at the head of three hundred men from Castleton and reached Ticonderoga on May 10.[26]

They advanced to the gateway—Arnold and Allen entering side by side. A sentinel snapped his fusee at Allen and retreated. Allen raced up the stairs and explained in a voice of thunder as he reached Commander William De La Place's room, "Come out here, you white-livered wretch, and surrender!"

The governor sat up, pale with terror, and stammered out, "In whose name do you demand it?"

"In the name," said Allen, "of the great Jehovah and the Continental Congress!"[27]

This was a high authority and the governor surrendered. They were equally successful in obtaining Crown Point. By this fortunate expedition, executed without bloodshed, they gained possession of two important fortresses, more than one hundred cannons, and a large quantity of ammunition. Congress knew nothing of the matter and did not commence their existence until some hours after they began their session. They chose Peyton Randolph president and Charles Thompson secretary, and each with a unanimous voice chose Rev. Jacob Duche to open the Congress with prayer. The complete command of Lake Champlain was of high importance to the Americans and could not be effective without their getting possession of a sloop of war. Arnold was chosen to sail her. He met up with Allen and Skeensborough was taken without bloodshed.

Let's move to Massachusetts.

Mr. John Hancock had been chosen at the last election—December 5, 1774—as president of the Provincial Congress and Dr. Joseph Warren chosen president of the Provincial Congress pro tempore. Meanwhile the inhabitants of Boston were forced to house General Gage's troops. A circular letter was written to the several towns of the colony stating:

> We conjure you by all that is dear, by all that is sacred, that you give all assistance possible informing the army. Our all is at stake. Death and devastation are the certain consequences of delay. Every moment is infinitely precious. An hour lost may deluge your country in blood, and entail perpetual slavery upon the few of your prosperity, who may survive the carnage. We beg and entreat, that you will answer it to your country; to your conscience, and above all as you will answer it to God himself, that you will hasten and encourage, by all possible means, the enlistment of men to form the army; and send them forward to headquarters at Cambridge, with that expedition which the vast importance and instant urgency of the affair demand.[28]

This address was attended to; the men discovered a readiness to turn out for the salvation of their country and the women applied themselves with cheerfulness to the fitting out of their husbands, fathers, brothers, and sons for the important expedition, while the dangers of it were overlooked or ignored.

Behold the bloodlines of the American soldier's families.

The Massachusetts Congress gathered the five thousand poor and Negroes out of Boston and sent them to different towns to keep them out of harm's way. Rhode Island and Connecticut made paper money to furnish a plentiful substitute for cash. The men coming from these colonies for the defense of Massachusetts were supplied with this money and would be credited for all payments.

On May 10, the Continental Congress again assembled at Philadelphia and issued bills of credit in the amount of $3 million, for defraying the expenses of the war, and pledged the faith of the

United Colonies for their redemption. This was an act of hope, as there was no gold to back the paper money.

They resolved upon a letter to the eastern tribe of Indians to secure their friendship and engage them on the side of the colonies. But let us remember that the Iroquois would take part with one side or the other; having a restless warlike temper, they were not in common disposed to observe neutrality. Most of the tribes sided with Britain because they were promised land, but the Oneidas, at first, wanted to stay neutral; they later joined with the colonists. The day the proclamation appeared, the chiefs and the warriors of the Oneida directed the following speech.

> We Oneidas are induced to this measure on account of the disagreeable situation of affairs and we hope by the help of God, the unhappy indifferences between you and Old England can be resolved. This has greatly troubled our minds. Possess your minds in peace respecting us. We cannot meddle in this dispute between two brothers. This quarrel seems unnatural. You are two brothers of one blood. We are unwilling to join on either side, for we bear equal affection to both Old and New England. We are for peace and we have declared our minds and desire you not apply to your Indian brethren for their assistance.
>
> Signed: William Sunogbsba, William Kanagbquaesea, Peter Thayebeare, Jimmy Tekayabeare, Nickbis Agbsenbare — garter; Thomas Yogbtanowea — spreading the dew; Adam Obonwana, Quedellis Agwerondongwas — breaking of the twig; Handerbeks Tegabsweabdyen — a belt (of wampum) extended; Jobnko Skeanendon & Thomas Teondeatha — a fallen tree.[29]

In May, the British army in Boston received reinforcements from England under Generals William Howe, Henry Clinton, and John Burgoyne, who, together with the garrison, formed an army of more than twelve thousand men. General Gage now proclaimed martial law throughout the State, offering, however, to pardon all rebels who would return to their allegiance—excepting Samuel Adams and John Hancock. The poor and the elderly inhabitants, plus the Negroes, who were in the process of leaving, were halted and were treated in a deplorable manner. The truth is, after a number had left, a clamor was raised by persons who were affected to the British government, alleged that as soon as the allowed-to-leave persons were safe, the town would be set on fire. Gage was so averse to allowing women and children to leave—even though he thought no real danger existed—he instead sent out the poor and helpless, *first infecting some of them with smallpox.*[30]

The Americans, learning that General Gage was determined to penetrate into the country by the way of Charleston Neck, issued orders to Col. William Prescott on the evening of June 16, to take one thousand men and form an entrenchment on Bunker Hill., an eminence that commanded the neck of the peninsula of Charlestown. By some mistake, they went farther on and occupied Breed's Hill. At midnight those stern-hearted men stood on the top while Putnam marked out the line of entrenchments. By daylight, they had constructed a redoubt eight rods square, in which they could shelter themselves.

In the morning the English officers and the Bostonians could hardly believe their eyes as they saw this redoubt almost over their heads. In two hours all artillery was pointed against that single silent structure. The city shook with the thunder of cannon, rocking the lonely height; still, those hardy men toiled on, heedless of the iron storm around them.

The cannonading failed to dislodge them. At about noon, Gen. Gage sent a body of about three thousand men, under Generals Howe and William Pigot, to carry the height of the assault. They left Boston in boats and, landing at Moreton's Point, advanced in two columns, setting fire to Charlestown on their way and leaving two thousand people deprived of their habitations.

The day was clear; not a cloud rested on the summer heavens. The soldiers on the hill gazed upon the moving mass below them with a stern and anxious eye. In the intervals of the roar of artillery were heard the thrilling strains of martial music, while plumes danced, standards danced, and three thousand bayonets gleamed and shook over the dark mass below.

A solitary horseman moved swiftly over the hill and rode up to Putnam. General Joseph Warren questioned, "Where will the onset be heaviest?"

"At the redoubt," replied Putnam. "Prescott is there."

Away galloped Warren, and as he rode up to the entrenchment a loud *huzza* filled the air.

Nothing could exceed the excitement of the scene at this moment; stretched over that hill, and out of sight, lay 1,500 sons of Liberty, coolly awaiting the onset of the veteran thousands of England, and sternly resolved to prove worthy of the high destinies entrusted to their charge. The roofs, steeples, and shores of Boston were black with spectators. Many of them had husbands, brothers, sons, and lovers on the hill. At home, an earnest prayer went up to heaven. With longing, each heart turned to the silent redoubt!

The English advanced. Putnam rode along the lines urging them not to fire until the command—and then aim at their waistbands. On came the battalions, stopping every few yards to deliver their deep and regular volleys on the embankments; not a shot replied, but flashing eyes were bent in wrath on the enemy as they slowly ascended the hill and sternly closed for the death struggle. That silence was more awful than the thunder of cannon—it told of carnage and death slumbering there.

When the hostile columns had almost reached the entrenchments, the stern order "Fire!" rang with startling clearness on the air. A sheet of flame burst along that low, dark wall and down went the enemy rank on rank as that tempest of fire smote their bosoms; still, the battalions struggled against the deadly sleet, but all in vain. Furious with rage, the army broke and fled for the shore. A loud huzza rose from the redoubt, which was answered by thousands of voices from Boston.

The English officers succeeded in rallying their ranks, and again they pressed forward only to meet another tempest of fire and lead. Again the English's bravest gave way and they rushed furiously back down the hill. Again the triumphant huzzas rocked the height and the slopes of the hill turned red with flowing blood.

At this critical moment, Gen. Clinton arrived, and by his exertions, the troops were again rallied and a third time advanced to the charge. Only one volley smote them as the Americans had fired their last cartridge and were without bayonets. Clubbing their muskets, they still beat back the enemy till the order to retreat was given. Putnam did not want to retreat and attempted to rally them. His efforts were in vain, he spewed a torrent of indignations, and Warren, too, urged them to another effort. An English officer recognized him, grabbed a musket, and shot him dead.

The Americans retreated with little loss across Charlestown Neck and finally took up station on Winter and Prospect Hills, still maintaining the command of the entrance to Boston.

The battlefield remained in the hands of the English, but the victory was ours. It had been a bloody day. Nearly two thousand slept in death on that hill, 1,500 of which were British soldiers. The news spread rapidly, and one long shout went up from every corner of the land.

In the meantime, Congress had assembled in Philadelphia. Once more they addressed letters to the king, the people of Great Britain and Ireland, and at the same time published to the world the reason of their appeal to arms. On June 15, 1775, Congress elected George Washington by unanimous vote to the high office of commander-in-chief of the United Colonies and voted to raise an army of twenty thousand men. Washington, who was present, accepted but addressed Congress:

> Mr. President:
> Though I am truly sensible of the high honor done me in this appointment, yet I feel distressed from a consciousness, that my abilities and military experience may not be equal to the extensive and important trust. However, as the Congress desire it, i will enter upon the momentous duty, and exert every power I possess in their service, and for the support of the glorious cause. I beg they will accept my most

cordial thanks for this distinguished testimony of their approbation. But lest some unlucky event should happen unfavorable to my reputation, I beg it may be remembered by every gentleman in the room, that this day declare, with the utmost sincerity, I do not think myself equal to the command I am honored with. As to pay, Sir, 1 beg leave to assure the Congress that as no pecuniary consideration could have tempted me to accept this arduous employment, at the expense of my domestic case and happiness, I do not wish to make any profit from it. I will keep an exact account of my expenses. Those, I doubt not, they will discharge, and that is all I desire.

G Washington[31]

In subordination to the commander-in-chief, Messrs. Artemus Ward, Charles Lee, Phillip John Schuyler, and Israel Putnam were appointed major-generals; Horatio Gates adjutant-general; Messrs. John Pomeroy, Richard Montgomery, and David Wooster; William Heath, Asa Spencer, Thomas Mifflin, John Sullivan, and Nathaniel Greene—brigadier-generals.

Soon after his election, General Washington, accompanied by Lee, proceeded to Cambridge to take command of the army, which amounted to about fourteen thousand men. He found them full of love for their country but without tents and ammunition, destitute of discipline, and adverse to subordination. By his own energy and the assistance of Gates, order and discipline were soon introduced and stores were collected, as well as everything needed for carrying on operations.

In July, Georgia chose delegates to Congress, increasing the number of the United Colonies to thirteen.

The British army was now closely blockaded in Boston and Congress resolved to seize the opportunity of sending a force into Canada, thus anticipating Sir Guy Carlton, the governor of that providence, who was evidently preparing to attack the colonies.

The army of the invasion consisted of about three thousand men. Two expeditions were planned: one by the way of Lake

Champlain, under the command of Gen. Schuyler and aided by Generals Montgomery and Wooster; the other by the way of the river Kennebec, under the command of Arnold.

Arnold's march of about for, days through the wilderness—at the head of more than one thousand men—is one of the most stupendous things in the annals of war. He marched more than two hundred miles through a forest, climbing mountains and scaling precipices, enduring toil, cold, and hunger.

On November 9, Arnold arrived at Point Levi, opposite Quebec, and sent a summons to the commander to surrender, which was treated with scorn. Arnold retreated twenty miles to wait for Montgomery.

Montgomery arrived in December 1, but the army was in a miserable condition. Fatigue, smallpox, and the severity of winter had taken a toll and they were poorly prepared to take a place like Quebec. After a siege of three weeks, facing a heavy snowstorm, a noble attempt by Montgomery had him moving snow by hand and struggling through. With the up-raised sword, he advanced through the picket and the gunners fled. His army found his lifeless body and the order to retreat had them fleeing the scene. One boyish form stood by the lifeless body of Montgomery, his eyes wet with tears. That fair boy, covered with the blood of a fight, was he who was almost President and emperor of Mexico—Aaron Burr.

Arnold retired his repulse three miles below Quebec, staying through winter till English reinforcements arrived on June 18, and the Americans made a hasty evacuation from Canada. The expedition ended in failure but well for our independence, as the protection of the providence would have drawn too many men from more important colonies.

While these events happened on the northern frontiers, English ships were laying waste to cities and towns upon our Atlantic coast. Bristol in Rhode Island and Falmouth in Massachusetts were burned by order of Capt. Henry Mowatt of the British navy because they had taken part in the rebellion. Congress thought it time to turn its attention to the construction of armed vessels. Thirteen were fitted, a navy established, and a large number of privateers licensed, which scoured the seas and did great injury to English commerce.

Gen. Washington employed in the service several cruisers to intercept the store ships of the enemy. Rewards were paid and regular courts of Admiralty were established for the adjudication of prizes, and by these timely measures, much good was accomplished.

One of the most fortunate leaders of these enterprises was Capt. John Manly of Marblehead. He captured an English ship loaded with ordnance stores and ammunition of immense value at the time. Among them was a large brass mortar on new construction, which he called the Congress. An invoice could scarcely have been formed of articles better suited to the pressing wants and circumstances of the army.

The distresses of the Bostonians and the English troops there exceeded the possibility of description. They were almost in a state of starvation and suffering for want of fuel. The wretched inhabitants were totally destitute of vegetables, flour, or fresh provisions and had to resort to feeding on horseflesh. A number of houses were taken down and used for fuel.

Efforts were still made by the British ministry to detach New York from the confederacy and to retain the colony under its influence. To this end, the ministry restored Gov. William Tryon, who was beloved by the people and empowered him to make use of measures to bribe and corrupt in various ways. Congress immediately recommended, *"All persons, whose going at large would endanger the liberty of America, should be arrested and secured."*

On hearing this Tryon took refuge on a ship in the harbor.

Virginia, during this year, was involved in difficulty through the insolent conduct of the royal governor, John Murray—Lord Dunmore. The government of Virginia was now in the hands of the colonial assembly, but Lord Dunmore, who had retired to the king's ship, did not abandon all hope of regaining his former station, and in November he issued proclamations, instituting martial law and promised freedom to such Negroes as would leave their masters and join his party. Many loyalists and Negroes joined his numbers when Dunmore left his ship and occupied a strong position near Norfolk. The Virginians took post nearly opposite of his.

Dunmore, being completely defeated, again returned to his ships, where, with his party of loyalists, he became reduced to great distress for want of provisions. He sent a flag to Norfolk, demanding a supply for his Majesty's ships, which was refused by the provincial commander; he set fire to Norfolk and reduced it to ashes.

By this inhuman act, nearly six thousand persons were deprived of habitations and three hundred pieces of sterling were lost.

At length, Dunmore was obliged to relinquish all attempts to regain his government and finally, after suffering from famine, tempest, and disease, sought refuge in the Southern Islands.

An act was passed that prohibited all trade and commerce with the colonies and authorized that the capture of all American and other vessels found trading with the colonies and the crews of these captured were to be treated not as prisoners but as slaves.

The colonists had sent over their last petition-styled the *Olive Branch*—to the king, but both houses of parliament refused to hear what they alleged coming from an unlawful assembly. Until now the American colonists had hoped for reconciliation with the mother country. This rejection was enough and it was determined this was the eternal separation of Great Britain and the colonies—the suppliants were suppliants no longer. *The flag, which had hitherto been plain red, was changed to thirteen stripes, emblematical of the union of the colonies.*[32]

At the close of this year (1775), the American army was almost entirely destitute of the supplies necessary for carrying on the war and the terms for enlistment for all the troops expired within the year. Although active measures had been taken for enlisting troops, on the last day of December when the old troops were to be disbanded, there were but 9,650 men enlisted for the ensuing year.

CAMPAIGN OF 1776

General Washington continued the blockade of Boston during the winter of 1775-76 and at last, resolved to bring the enemy to action. It was thought expedient to fortify Dorchester Heights, which commanded the harbor and British shipping. The night of March 4 was selected for the attempt, and a bright full moon favored them in their toilsome employment. The amount of labor performed through the night, considering the depth of the frozen earth, was incredible. Great preparations were made to defend themselves from the raking fire they expected from the enemy's ships. George Washington was present, animating the soldiers, and they, in turn, manifested warm hearts in the service.

The surprise of the British the next morning cannot easily he conceived. A few moments sufficed to tell Gen. Howe the advantage the Americans had gained, and no alternative remained for him but to dislodge them or retire, for his vessels were too exposed to remain in the harbor. It was his wish to attack the Americans, but a violent tempest of wind and rain came on the night after and obliged him to abandon his enterprise. The Americans looked on this as the work of divine Providence, who, by forming this frustrating design, had stopped what would have been an enterprise of immense slaughter.

On the morning of March 17, the royal army comminced its embarkation, and the inhabitants beheld, with great joy, the whole fleet under sail.

By this event, they were relieved from a force of 7,575 regulars, exclusive of staff, which, with the marines and sailors, may be estimated at about ten thousand in the whole.

This force greatly exceeded the five regiments, which Gen. James Grant boasted in England that he could march successfully from one end of the American continent to the other. Fifteen hundred Tories left the country with their families on board the transports with the army, not knowing what part of the world would be their home.

The houses and streets of Boston presented a deplorable scene to the army as they entered. Wretchedness and desolation were written on every side and reflected disgrace on the late occupants.

A spacious brick building that for more than a century had been consecrated to the service of God was occupied as a riding school for Burgoyne's regiment of dragoons. A beautiful pew, carved and finished in silk, was used as a fence for a hog sty.[33]

General Washington requested the Rev. Dr. Eliot preach a thanksgiving sermon. On November 28, taking from Isaiah 33:20, in the presence of his Excellency and a numerous audience, Rev. Eliot offered thanks to the Providence for their successes.

The remains of Major Warren, hero and patriot, were taken from the earth at Breed's Hill by the Lodge of the Free Masons, where he was the late Grand Master, and buried in the usual funeral solemnities of that society, attended by the grand procession of the society. After the eulogy was pronounced, the remains were placed in the the vault under the chapel. The port of Boston was now again opened, having been closed for two years by order of an act of the British parliament.

The British counted on to expeditions for the campaign of 1776. Besides the relief of Quebec and the recovery of Canada, the object of one expedition was to reduce the southern colonies with the command given to Gen. Henry Clinton and Sir Peter Parker. The object of the other was to gain possession of New York, this object is given to the successors of Gen. Gage and Sir William Howe.

During this time the most melancholy accounts were received from the army in Canada; they were subjected to hardships, suffering, and destitute of provisions, sinking under fatigue and reduced by smallpox. Reinforcements had been ordered by Congress, but when they arrived they were worn out and sinking under disease.

General John Thomas succeeded Arnold in the command. He sent a fireship down the St. Lawrence to destroy the governor's vessels, but the plan was discovered and on that very day several British ships arrived and cut off all communication. Gen. Thomas was obliged to retreat.

Many of the sick fell into the hands of Gen. John Thomas who treated them with great kindness. After a forty-five-mile march, he too succumbed to the disease, and the command went to Gen. Sullivan.

British forces in Canada now numbered thirteen thousand. The general place of rendezvous was Three Rivers, but a party under Gen. Barry St. Leger was near them on a transport, and another with Generals John Burgoyne, Christopher Carleton, William Phillips, and Baron Friedrich Adolph Riedesel was on the march from Quebec.

Adverse fortune followed the Americans in every part of Canada. Gen. Sullivan received order to embark on the lakes for Crown Point and thus ended the bold but unsuccessful attempt to annex Canada to the United Colonies.[34]

An official letter had been intercepted early in that year, announcing the departure of a large armament from England under Sir Peter Parker and Gen. Clinton; its destination being against the Southern States. Forthwith the gallant Southerners began to prepare for its reception. The only resistance the inhabitants of Charleston could make was to defend Sullivan's Island, and the militia of the country was summoned to surround the capital.

Palmetto trees, which resemble the cork, had been cut in the forest, and the logs in immense rafts were moored to the beach. With these huge palmettos, a square pen was made with bastions at the angles, capable of covering one thousand men. When completed it presented the appearance of a solid wall sixteen feet wide.

Although ignorant of gunnery, these valiant men, nerved with courage, were confident of success and toiled on their preparations. The command of this fort was given to Col. William Moultrie. Behind it he placed 435 brave soldiers with thirty-one cannon, the total caliber of which was about 535 pounds. Much had been said to Col. Moultrie in derision of this rudely built affair. A former captain of an English man-of-war warned them in the most emphatic manner, saying to Col. Moultrie, "Sir, when the enemy's ship come to lay alongside of your fort, they will knock it down in half an hour."

Moultrie very coolly replied, "Then we will lie behind the ruins, and prevent the men from landing."

General Charles Lee, whose eye had been accustomed to the scientific structures of Europe, requested the governor to have it immediately evacuated; but looking proudly on the brave men who had sworn to protect it, Gov. Edward Rutledge replied, "I would never give my sanction to such an order while a soldier remained alive to defend it."

The sequel will tell how bravely they kept their determination.

On the morning of June 28, a detachment from the fleet, consisting of nvo ships of fifty guns each, five of twenty-six, one of twenty-six, and a bomb vessel, came steadily up, driven by a fair wind. As they neared the fort, Col. Moultrie's eyes flashed with delight, and he gave orders to his men to fire. That bold onset was in earnest of what followed. Not a shot was returned from the fleet until they cast anchors directly abreast of the fort, when a fearful volley from more than one hundred cannon greeted them, and the battle had fairly commenced.

General Lee had stationed himself at Haddrell's Point, expecting to see the fort shattered into fragments in thirty minutes. Hour after hour passed, during which time the firing seemed like one constant peal of thunder; the fort trembled at times like a frightened thing, as hundreds of balls buried themselves in the good palmettos. Lee passed over to the fort in an open boat, amazed that an English fleet of 266 guns should be kept at bay by thirty-one cannon and four hundred inexperienced artillerists.

His astonishment increased as he gazed upon the coolness and intrepidity of those noble men. Finding his presence of no avail, he left the fort and returned to his old station. An incessant shower of bombs flew through the air, and quantities dropping within the fort were lost in the morass in the middle. With joy they saw the bomb vessel rendered useless, and every succeeding discharge after told with murderous effect.

During the heat of the battle, the flagstaff was shot away, and the flag dropped on the beach. A deep groan of despair was heard from hundreds of the citizens of Charleston who had crowded the wharves and steeples and were watching with intense anxiety the event of the battle. Every face grew pale as the flag disappeared, and many an eye filled with tears.

The firing continued; the sky was ablaze, and the smoke billowed, and thunder answered from the sea. A few moments elapsed, and they saw the flag shaking its folds in the breeze from its former place. Among the bravest of those brave ones within the fort was Sergeant William Jasper. Quickly he sprang from one of the embrasures, snatched the dripping flag from the ditch, and walking the whole length of the works, the halls falling fearfully around him, coolly mounted the logs and supported the flag upon the parapet until another staff was procured. From the citizens on the wharves and the heights of Charleston, a shout of joy rang out.

All day long beneath a burning sky, they fought without cessation, and when the level beams of the setting sun lighted the sea, the battle still raged furiously. Slowly, says one in graphic style, the grey twilight began to creep over the water, and at last darkness settled on the shores and the sea. The scene became one of indescribable grandeur; heavy cannonade continued and still the spectators who lined the mainland gazed seaward through the gloom toward the spot where the combat raged.[35]

Night had fallen on the island and fort, and all was dark and invisible there, except when the flash of the guns lit up its form. Then its mysterious bosom for a moment would be inherent with flame, and it seemed as if the sea itself had opened and shot forth fire. Around those ships the smoke lay like a heavy storm cloud, through which the lightning incessantly played and thunder roared. Moultrie and his men could hear the heavy blows of their shot as they struck the ships and crashed through the solid timbers.

Finally, the English, despairing of conquering such men, moved quietly away, and Marion *(who* would play *such* a brave roll) fired the last gun as the ships were retiring, as a parting salute, and so well aimed that it struck the cabin of the commander's ship, killing two officers and three sailors.

All through the streets of Charleston one loud huzza echoed, "Victory! Victory!" While from the little palmetto fort, three hearty cheers replied and thereafter it was named in honor of its gallant defender, Fort Moultrie. Oooh-rah!³⁶

(Anti-war activists and liberal whiners pay heed.)

They mourned over the dead bodies of ten of their band, but they grieved as for brave men who died in the service of their country fighting for liberty. Twenty-two were wounded, while the loss of the British was about 171 dead and sixty wounded. A number of officers were slain and their ships shattered almost to perfect ruin.³⁷

A few days after this brilliant action, Gov. Rutledge and *many* of the fair women of Charleston visited the bold soldiers at the fort. The gallant Jasper was brought forward, and as a reward for his chivalric act of replacing the flag on the parapet, Gov. Rutledge buckled his own sword around the stalwart form, while a pair of elegantly-embroidered colors were presented to Moultrie's regiment by Mrs. Elliot. After a few words, she begged them to accept the colors.

"I make not the least doubt, under Heaven's protection, and you will stand by them as long as they can wave in the air of Liberty."³⁸

Jasper heard this speech and remembered it well.

Sometime after, during the assault on Savannah, Jasper received a mortal wound while in the act of replacing those colors on the parapet of the Springhill redoubt. Feeling the damp dew of death gathering on his brow, he summoned his companions in war about him to hear his last words.

Said he, "I have got my furlough. Governor Rutledge presented this sword to me in the defense of Fort Moultrie. Give it to my father and tell him 1 have worn it with honor. If he should weep, tell him his son died in hope of a better life. Tell Mrs. Elliot that I have given my life, supporting the colors which she presented to our regiment."

He then sent a message to a Mrs. Jones, whose husband he had rescued with much bravery from the enemy, saying, "When Jones returns to you, his wife and son, tell him that Jasper is gone, but the remembrance of the battle which we fought brought a secret joy to my heart, when it was about to stop its motion forever." He expired a few minutes after closing his last sentence.

The remainder of the fleet set sail for the North, where the whole of the British fleet had been ordered to assemble.

During these transactions at the South, the Continental Congress was in session, watching with anxiety the aspect of affairs in both countries and revolving the chances for success in the approaching contest. Upon the first intelligence received at Philadelphia of the troops to be employed against the Americans, a citizen of eminence wrote to his correspondent, "We now know who the commissioners are, and their numbers, viz. Messrs. the Hessians, Brunswickers, Waldcckers, English, Scotch and Irish. This gives the coup de grace to the British and American connection. It has already wrought wonders in this city; conversations have been more rapid than ever under Mr. Whitfield. The Pennsylvania farmer (John Dickinson) told me yesterday in the field-that his sentiments were changed-he had been desirous to keep the door open as long as possible and was now convinced that nothing was to be expected from our enemies but slavery.

In the first week in June, Richard Henry Lee, one of the deputies from Virginia, made a motion in Congress to declare the American colonies free and independent states, followed by an eloquent speech, which found and echoed in many hearts. It was further discussed on the of June, when it was postponed for subsequent consideration until the first day of July, voting that at the same time a committee be appointed to propose a full declaration.

The committee was elected by ballot and consisted of Thomas Jefferson, John Adams, Benjamin Franklin, Roger Sherman, and Robert Livingston.

Mr. Jefferson and Mr. Adams acted as a subcommittee to prepare the draft and Mr. Jefferson drew up the paper. The merit of this document is Mr. Jefferson's. Some changes were made in it on the suggestion of other members of the committee and by others in Congress while it was under discussion.

On the 4th of July 1776, upon the report of the committee, the thirteen confederate colonies dissolved their allegiance to the British crown and boldly declared themselves free and independent under the name of the Thirteen United States of America.[39]

In their declaration they boldly expressed the grievances and oppression for which they could not receive redress and proclaimed to the world the causes that impelled them to a separation from the Crown of Great Britain.

According to recommendations of Congress, those colonies that had not yet adopted constitutions were advised to establish "such governments as might best conduce to the happiness and safety of the people." The colonies had been accustomed to look upon themselves as sovereign States; and the recommendation was generally complied with, and the government was in every instance entirely elective and at such short periods as to impress upon the rulers their immediate accountableness to the people.

The subject of independence had for some time agitated the public mind, and various opinions were entertained relative to that momentous transaction. Some objections were raised, as it was considered doubtful whether the grand object-liberty-could be gained. And when we reflect on the deranged condition of the army, the fearful deficiency of resources, and the little prospect of foreign assistance, and at the same time contemplate the prodigious powers and resources of the enemy, we look with wonder upon this bold measure of Congress.

It has been said that the history of the world cannot furnish an instance of fortitude and heroic magnanimity parallel to that displayed by the members whose signatures are affixed to the Declaration of American Independence. Their venerated names will ornament the brightest pages of American history and be transmitted to the latest generations.

A signature to this paper would he regarded in England as treason and expose them to the halter or the block. These brave men knew well what an ignominious death awaited them in case their experiment failed. But they had counted the cost and realized the responsibility of their station. As a nation, the American people, in their helplessness, bowed before the omnipotent Ruler of the world and besought His protection and guidance. They felt their cause was just, they were oppressed in their dearest rights and privileges, and they hesitated not to appeal to heaven for aid.

The President of Congress, John Hancock, led the way in this bold work, and the original paper still exhibit's the characters written by no coward's hand. Of all the fifty-six signers, but one hand trembled as he signed what might have proved his own death warrant. The name of Stephen Hopkins is traced in trembling lines owing to a severe attack of palsy of which he was afflicted.[40]

The pen lies safe in Massachusetts; all who signed have passed to the ages. Their bodies rest, but their example, in the recorded proofs of their own noble actions, principles, and opinions, will for succeeding generations act upon the affairs of men throughout the civilized world.

Charles Carroll of Carrolton, Maryland, was the last of this venerable body to survive. He lived to see one after another leave this world; the longevity of the signers has been frequently noticed. The average lives of the New England delegation (fourteen in number) was seventy-five years. Four of the others lived to the age of ninety and upward; fourteen exceeded eighty years, and most of the others reached the age of three-score years and ten. They had lived to see the goodness of the Lord in granting them from oppression, and in their advanced age could hear testimony to their posterity, that God was the hearer and answerer of prayer.[41]

Voices of joy throughout the Union welcomed the Declaration. From old and young, master and servant, the glad tones were echoed that America was, and of a right ought to be, a free and independent nation.

In Virginia the rejoicing was almost beyond description. The name of King George was suppressed in all public prayers, and the great seal of the commonwealth was drawn to represent Virtue as the tutelary genius of province, trampling on the tyranny of the monarchy, which was represented by the figure of a prostrate man whose crown had fallen from his head, bearing in one hand a scourge and the other a chain. The words *Sic Semper Tyrannis* (Thus Always to Tyrants) inscribed, circling around the effigy of Virtue. On the reverse, representing Liberty with her wand and cap, was Ceres, with the horn of plenty in one hand and a sheath of wheat in the other, and at the bottom these words were inscribed: Deus Noblis Hae Otia Fecit (God Has Given Us Tranquility).

In New York, the leaden statue of George Ill was taken down and converted into bullets.

In Boston, thirteen salutes, corresponding to the number of American States, were fired, and King Street received the name of State Street. The bells rang out a joyous peal, while members of council and the House of Representatives, magistrates, clergymen, and selectmen all assembled to hear the news proclaimed, and in the loud huzzas from the concourse of people, every voice joined. After ensigns of royalty, lions, crowns, and scepters were destroyed, the people felt they were forever absolved from all allegiance to a tyrant's throne.

The British ministry was confounded at what it called the daring enormity of the colonists in spurning its mighty power and authority. The ministry was surprised the rebels dared to show such temper and spirit. Forthwith they determined to deploy augmented forces to crush them at a blow, and to coerce them into a sense of duty and submission to their king.

Doubting the competency of their own power to subjugate the colonies, the English parliament, at an immense expense, resorted to the aid of foreign troops to prosecute their bloody work. They entered into a treaty with several German princes to furnish seventeen thousand men to aid in reducing the Americans to vassalage. Besides the wages, terms of the treaties included 30 sterling paid for each soldier slain and fifteen for each disabled. The total expense for these foreign troops was not less than 1,500,000 for one year.

With a horde of foreign soldiers, Lord Howe and Gen. Howe, with power to restore peace and grant pardons to "his majesty's subjects" that deserved clemency, landed July 12 at Staten Island. Gen. Clinton, who had his behind handed to him by the Charleston militia, limped his shattered ship in soon after. Gen. Howe, who had fled Boston, had arrived July 2, so that in total the British forces numbered thirty-five thousand.

June had Howe offering his proclamation of pardon, which Congress boldly caused to he printed with accompanying remarks, showing the people its insidious nature, and advising them to he true to their own cause.

The commissioners then dispatched Col. John Henry Patterson, adjutant-general of the British army, to General Washington at New York with letters respecting their mission, but as the letters were not directed in a manner expressive of his official capacity; he refused to receive them.

In a few days, Patterson again sent General Washington a letter addressed and directed to *George Washington, Esq. &c, &c, &c.,* hoping the three etceteras would remove all difficulty.

General Washington absolutely declined receiving this letter, adding that &c could mean everything or might mean anything. All public letters must be directed to him according to his rank.

Col. Patterson then said that the letters contained offers of pardon, &c, to which General Washington coolly replied, "The Americans committed no wrong, and therefore wanted no pardon; they were defending what they deemed their indisputable rights."[42]

Col. Patterson manifested great solicitude that the letters might be received and reconciliation could take place. General Washington with firmness and dignity refused.

Washington was well assured that warlike operations would speedily follow, and forthwith preparations were made to fortify New York and increase the army. The possession of New York was a favorite object of the British, on account of its central situation and the ease with which possession could he maintained. In April, General Washington had fixed his headquarters in the city and endeavored by any means in his power to prepare for its defense.

The Continental Army numbered only 10,514 effective soldiers, and these were so circumstanced that but a small part could be brought into action. Thirteen thousand troops were ordered to join the army, which, with the invalids and men destitute of arms, would increase in number to twenty-seven thousand.

(American soldiers would drag themselves on elbows to defend America. The British did not have a chance.)

On August 22, the British forces landed on the southern shores of Long Island, causing the inhabitants to flee in terror, burning their own houses and stores to prevent them from becoming British property.

The British were seen advancing on the roads and the American troops were drawn up to meet them. This was a feint by the enemy to divert attention from the main body made up by Hessians. The Americans fought bravely then another approach of British troops passed around to the left to cut off any retreat and instead forced them back into the Hessians.

For six hours several regiment of Americans fought in this desperate manner, but being ignorant of Gen. Clinton's action had their retreat intercepted. Many, however, broke through and escaped the lines.

The Americans defended themselves with great bravery but were unequal to the contest. The British possessed the most decided advantage in numbers, artillery, discipline, and experience. That Washington should be able to keep the field at all with these ever-shifting, undisciplined, unfinished troops has been proclaimed a miracle of the Providence.

In this instance British discipline triumphed over the mere desperation and bravery of raw troops, whose officers were not even acquainted with the science of war. The American loss was one thousand. Among the prisoners were Generals Sullivan and William A. Stirling, and eighty-two other officers of various ranks. The British loss was 450.

This battle was considered the most unskilled and imprudent one fought during the war. Had the British shown sufficient energy, all the Americans might have been secured or slain. The battle was fought against the advice and wish of Washington, and but for his consummate skill and energy, the whole army would have been lost.

During the engagement, General Washington crossed over from New York to Brooklyn, and his stout heart was moved to anguish on seeing so many of his best men slaughtered. Had he in his moment of affliction acted on impulse or for vainglory, he might have drawn all his troops from New York, but on mature deliberation he decided to preserve his army for the future.

Gen. Nathaniel Greene, tossing on his sick bed (his regiment had met the Hessians under Putnam), his brave heart wrung with sorrow as he was told his regiment had been mishandled and cut to ribbons, burst into an agony of tears.

After this distressing defeat, our army retreated within their lines at Brooklyn and was exposed to the greatest hazard-fatigue. They were discouraged by defeat, a superior enemy in their front, and a powerful fleet about to enter the East River; the care of Providence and the wisdom of Washington preserved them from destruction.

Having resolved to withdraw his troops from their hazardous position, he crossed over to the island on the night of August 29' and in person conducted the retreat in so successful a manner, under circumstances the most trying, that it is considered a remarkable example of good generalship. The circumstance, which is remarked as manifestly Providential, is that a thick fog enveloped the whole of Long Island in obscurity at about two in the morning, which at this season of the year was quite unusual. The atmosphere on the opposite bank was perfectly clear.

Prayer does work wonders.

About eight in the evening, the troops began to move when a violent northeast wind and the ebb tide prevented them from leaving. Many hearts beat rapidly when suddenly the wind veered to the northwest and immediately they wafted over and landed in New York.

Never was any movement more manifestly favored by Providence, and the Americans felt and openly acknowledged the special care of God in so singly favoring their safe retreat. The wind changed exactly to their need, and the fog veiled them from an enemy so near that the sound of their pick-axes was plainly heard.

The entire American army was conveyed over a river that was upwards of a mile wide and landed at New York in less than thirteen hours. After the last of the officers left the shore, a few minutes passed before the British entered.

Lord Richard Howe, supposing the hostile spirit of the rebels had been humbled by their defeat at the hand of his brother Sir William Howe, sent a letter to Congress requesting a conference with some members as private gentlemen. Accordingly, Dr. Franklin, John Adams, and Edward Rutledge were chosen to meet with Lord Howe on Staten Island. The first proposition of his lordship was that the colonies should return to their allegiance and obedience to the government of Great Britain. The committee replied, "It is not to be expected after the contempt with which our former humble positions have been treated; and it is not till the last act of parliament, which denounced war against us, and put us out of the king's protection, that we declared our independence, and now it is too late for oppressed and indignant people to return to a dependent state."[43] The committee conducted the business with great dignity and judgment.

General Washington, finding New York City an unsafe place, as he was in danger of being surrounded, retired with his entire army about nine miles to the north. This also was a hazardous undertaking; but he was allowed by a protecting Providence to affect it, though under a heavy cannonade from the British ships.

A circumstance occurred on the route. Maj-Gen. Putnam, last leaving with 3,500 continental troops, chose a parallel road unknowing that eight thousand British troops were advancing on the same road. Most fortunately they saw no prospect of engaging our troops and instead chose to retire to the mansion of Mr. Robert Murray, a firm supporter of American independence. Mrs. Mary Murray offered them wine and cake, and they tarried for hours. Ten minutes more would have put our weary troops encountering the superior force again. Mrs. Murray was often afterward noticed as saving the American army.

The enemy immediately took possession of the city, and a destructive fire broke out consuming one thousand homes. It was estimated that about one fourth of the city was laid to waste. The Loyalists, or Tories, were suspected of the devastation.

About this time Captain Nathan Hale, a highly interesting young officer from Connecticut, learning Washington wished to ascertain the state of the British army on Long Island, volunteered for the dangerous service of a spy. He entered the British army in disguise and obtained the desired information, but being apprehended in his attempt to return, he was carried before Howe and, by his orders, was executed the next morning. At the place of execution he explained, "I lament I have but one life to lay down for my country!"

Howe again tried to negotiate, but he could not promise the Americans their independence, and they would not accept any other terms. Still the prospects of the country were alarming. Until the check at Brooklyn, the thoughts of heaven constantly favoring their cause gave much hope, but everything appeared to threaten a total dissolution of the army.

The militia abandoned their colors by the hundreds, and entire regiments deserted and returned to their homes. Their engagements were but for a year or even a few weeks and the thought of returning home induced them to avoid danger. Washington strove earnestly, with promises, persuasions, and exhortations. If he did not succeed according to his desires, he obtained more than his hopes. To Congress he addressed an energetic picture of the deplorable state of the forces, and assured them he must despair of success unless furnished with an army that should stand by him. To affect this, a bounty of $50 was offered at the time of engagement, and portions of unoccupied land were promised to officers and soldiers.

But although Washington hoped to reap the benefits of these arrangements, time would have to intervene; and his present prospect was that of a handful of dispirited and ill-found troops contending against a large and victorious army. In this situation he adopted the policy to harass and wear out his enemy, without risking any general engagement-why he has been called the American Fabius.

Ever tried to kick a little, vicious dog? They can run in and bite your ankles numerous times and race away before you can stop the attack. Washington used the same tactics against the British.

A skirmish occurred on Sept. 16 when the British attempted to cut off the road from which Washington received his supplies, but he had already moved his camp, and although bloodshed did occur, the enemy failed of their object. With his supplies Washington moved to North Castle, crossed the Hudson, and took post near Fort Lee.

On November 16, Fort Washington was lost, but the two thousand troops crossed and joined Washington who, with the main army, removed to Newark, NJ.

Washington retreated across New Jersey with the British lumbering behind them and passed on through New Brunswick, Princeton, and Trenton. Here the British expected to seize their prey, but with a diligence and energy far exceeding theirs, the Americans had just crossed over, the last boat with the baggage still on the river when the enemy appeared on the opposite bank. Charles Cornwallis had no boats in which to cross the river. He waited for the river to freeze. The British had almost six times the strength to that of Washington's, but their inertness, and his great and skillful exertions, hindered their overtaking them. This seems clearly another of those cases of an interposing Providence.

Feeble as was the American army when Washington commenced his retreat, it had by the hour diminished. His troops were unfed, amidst fatigue, unshod, while their bleeding feet were forced over sharp projections of frozen ground and they endured the keen December air almost without clothes or tents. Washington, with the firmness of the commander united with the tenderness of the father, visited the sick, gave everything in his power to the wants of the army praised their constancy, represented their suffering to Congress, and encouraged their despairing minds by holding out prospects of a better future. Ever relying on God for support and direction, he moved calmly forward amid the darkest storms, assured that even defeat in battle, insults of foes, or ingratitude or treachery in friends, would eventually work together for good to those whose cause was blessed of God. Here we still behold Washington in this darkest hour in American history firmly trusting in an overruling Providence, calling on those around him to exercise the same faith, and cheering them in their toilsome marches.

The distress of the Americans was increased by the desertion of many of the supposed friends of their cause. Howe, taking advantage of what he considered their vanquished and hopeless condition, couched in a haughty style, demanding submission to the king's authority within sixty days from the date of the paper. Two of the members of the continental Congress, Mr. Joseph Galloway and Mr. Thomas Allen, accepted pardon and submitted to kingly rule. The *extremes of* society, the very rich (Hollywood-Democrat politicians, anti-war nuts) and the very poor (who expect the government to provide their every want and need as their right), sued for the royal clemency, but few of the middle-class deserted their country in its hour of peril, though told that the gallows would be the alternative.

Washington, in this emergency, called in the distant detachments of the army, and under Gen. Mifflin 1,500 militia joined him. He had ordered Gen. Charles Lee to go north, but Lee disobeyed, lingering in New Jersey. Day after day passed, and still no reinforcements appeared. At length he saw fit by slow marches to put his troops in motion, but on route, as just punishment for his disobedience, a party of British cavalry took him prisoner. Many suspicions were aroused by this singular event. Considering his deliberate disobedience in the moment of critical danger to the army and knowing the unbounded ambitions of Gen. Lee, there was no doubt but he delayed, hoping Washington and his dispirited band might fall into the hands of the enemy and the supreme command devolve on him. Gen. Lee was a man of great military experience; he had fought in European battles and knew perfectly well what belonged to every subordinate officer, and there was no greater form of disobedience than to refuse orders like those of Washington.

(We shall see, in this pursuit of history, how the wicked are punished from their own actions, while walking in accordance with the laws of God rewards the good.

Pay heed, those who sell your soul, lusting for power; your punishment awaits you.)

With these reinforcements the Army amounted to seven thousand effective men. Enlistment would expire at the end of the year and the cause of America demanded important use should be made of the short space. With these General Washington resolved with all the energy of his mighty spirit to make one fearful struggle. He dared not go into winter quarters in the midst of such a season of gloom, almost of despair.

ACTUAL EVENTS AT THE FAMOUS CROSSING OF THE DELAWARE

At Trenton, on the other side of the icy waters of the Delaware, were stationed 1,500 Hessians; while farther on, at different places, were several other detachments. General Washington determined to re-cross the Delaware and attack the British posts at Trenton and Burlington. Headley says that the noble form of Washington, on the night of December 25, just at dusk, stood on the shore of the Delaware. His horse, saddled and bridled, was near him, while all around were heard the rumbling of artillery wagons and the confused sounds of marching men and hasty orders. The deep sullen stream went swiftly by and the angry heavens betokened a cold and stormy night. As he stood there and watched, there stole over his majestic countenance a look of inexpressive calmness. Before the morning the fate of that gallant army would he fixed and the next rising sun would shine down on his country, either lifted from its depth of despondency, or sunk deeper in its ruin. Events, big with the fate of the army and the nation, were crowding to their development, and his soul was absorbed in their contemplation.[44]

At length the boats were launched. The night was dark and cold, and, just as if in harmony with the scene, a storm arose driving full into the soldiers' faces, and amid the roar of the wind and crashing of the ice were heard the loud words of command and shouts of the men. The boats were forced backward and forward by the icy fragments, became scattered in the gloom, and would have been thrown into confusion but for the friend of Washington Colonel Henry Knox, who, standing on the farther shore, kept shouting through the darkness with his booming voice, thus indicating the point for which they were to steer. There, too, stood Washington, hour after hour, with that strangely calm, yet determined face, while his soul was racked with anxiety as the night waned rapidly away, and his distracted *army* still struggled in the midst of the icy stream. All night long did he stand there on the frozen shore urging on his weary troops, looking anxiously at his watch, and striving to pierce the fog that covered the water. Finally at four o'clock in the morning, the crossover completed and the columns got on the way. It was still dark; a storm of snow and hail pelted their weary bodies; their clothes were soaked wet and the muskets most rendered unfit for use.

What was to be done?

Advance and charge!

Nearing the Hessian picket, Washington ordered the guns to be unlimbered and the whole column to advance. Still riding in the front where the first volley must fall, his friends became alarmed for his safety and urged him to fall back to a place of greater security. But he rode sternly forward amid their guns with the storm beating furiously on his noble brow, every lineament of his countenance revealing the unalterable purpose of his soul.

The thunder of cannon was now heard through the storm from Sullivan's division, John Stark's regiment had already broken into the street, and a battle shout brought the Hessians awake. All now was confusion, and just then, the enemy wheeled two cannon into the street up which the column of Washington was advancing. Young James Monroe, a future president, and Captain William Washington, relative of the commander in chief, immediately sprung forward with their men, charged up to the very muzzles and took them, although the lighted matches were already descending on the pieces. When the smoke lifted, these two gallant officers were seen reclining in the arms of their followers, wounded, though not mortally. The Americans pressed onward, bearing down all opposition, until the enemy, confused and terrified, struck their flags. At a gallop, Washington dashed forward, exclaiming to one of his officers, "This is a glorious day for our country!"

The surprised Hessian commander Gottlieb Rahl was mortally wounded; one thousand troops were taken prisoner, and Washington took the quarters. The Hessian prisoners were in morbid fear of the Americans. The British had told them that, if captured, the Americans would shove splinters of wood into their skin and set them on fire. This lie was so they would fight harder. Instead of the dreadful death, they were fed and treated with respect.[45]

Howe was thunderstruck at this astonishing reverse. Cornwallis, raging like a bull with intentions of giving battle to the Americans, arrived on the first of January. Washington blew the inferiority of his force and was sensible that flight would be almost as fatal to the republicans as defeat. About midnight, leaving the fires burning briskly that his army should not be missed, he silently decamped, by a circuitous route, to the rear of the enemy. At sunrise the van of the American forces unexpectedly met two British regiments that were on the march to join Cornwallis. A conflict ensued, the Americans gave way, and all was at stake. Washington himself, at this decisive moment, led on the main body. The enemy were routed and fled. Washington pressed forward toward Princeton where one enemy regiment remained. A part of these saved themselves by flight; the remainder were made prisoners. Thus Washington again had accomplished his objective.

Thrilling were the emotions with which these successes were hailed by a disheartened nation and from which, when an unexpected and joyful event is related, the speaker proclaims, *"Great news from the Jerseys!"*[46]

On hearing the cannonade, Cornwallis, apprehensive for the safety of New Brunswick, immediately put his army in motion for that place. Washington, somewhat refreshed, took the field and, having gained possession of Newark, Woodbridge, Elizabethtown, and all the enemy's posts in New Jersey except New Brunswick and Amboy, retired to secure winter quarters at Morristown.

Washington's military glory now rose to its meridian. Indeed nothing in the history of war shows a leader in a more advantageous point of light than the last events of this campaign. Hannibal made war for revenge, Caesar and Napoleon for ambition, Washington for justice-for the rights of his country and for mankind.

Congress in the meantime was surrounded with difficulties that would have utterly discouraged men of weaker heads or fainter hearts. They were without power, funds were exhausted to recruit an army, and they were almost out of credit.

To raise money they authorized a loan, created a lottery, and they sent three commissioners to France to borrow of that government. These commissioners, Benjamin Franklin, Silas Deane, and Arthur Lee, were also, if possible, to prevail upon the French government to acknowledge the American independence.

On April 25, two thousand men under Gov. William Tryon, commander of the Tories, having passed the sound, landed between Fairfield and Norwalk. The next day, proceeding to Danbury, they compelled the garrison, under Huntington, to retire, and not only destroyed the stores but burned the town. Meanwhile eight hundred militia collected to annoy them and five hundred, under Arnold, attacked their front; Wooster fell upon their rear. The cowards spent the night at Ridgefield, set fire to it, and, still retreating, harassed by Arnold at Campo, they hid on their ships.[47]

The British had collected at Sag Harbor on Long Island large magazines of forage and grain. Col. Jonathan Meigs left Guilford on May 23 with 170 men and destroyed the stores, burned a dozen brigs and sloops, and returned without loss.

Congress had, with great judgment, selected Dr. Benjamin Franklin as one of the missions to France. A profound knowledge of human nature had given to this philosopher a manner possessing a peculiar charm attractive to all, however different their taste of pursuits. He exerted these powers so successfully that he excited great interest at the court of France for the American cause.

Several gentlemen of rank and fortune came forward. The most distinguished of these was Gilbert Motier Marquis de La Fayette, a young nobleman who, although he had everything to attach him to his own country, took the resolution to risk his life and fortune for the cause of American liberty and human rights

La Fayette was told of the despairing state of the country; so poor that it could not provide him any monetary compensation. "Then," said La Fayette, "this is moment I can render the most essential service."[48]

He provided his own vessel, and his arrival caused heartfelt joy. Washington received him as a son, and Congress made him a major general.

The grand British plan was to send troops to Canada, the attacking from Lake Champlain and New York. It was supposed the east might thus divide from the south. Gen. Burgoyne was sent from England, arriving in May. His force consisted of 7,173 British, several thousand Canadians, and Indians. The Americans made a brave attempt but were forced to retreat. Burgoyne took possession of Skeeneshorough.

Gen. Schuyler moved the American troops to the mouth of the Mohawk. He had obstructed the roads by breaking the bridges and dropping immense trees across them. Benjamin Lincoln, Arnold, and Daniel Morgan were sent north, which encouraged volunteers to join. The celebrated patriot of Poland, Thaddeus Kosciusko, was the chief engineer of troops. Burgoyne was in need of supplies and, arriving at Fort Edward on July 30, learned of a large store and sent five hundred men to seize it.

General John Stark, with a body of New Hampshire and Vermont troops, was on the march to join Gen. Phillip Schuyler. He met a British force four miles from Bennington. The militia dispersed when five hundred British reinforcements arrived. The Green Mountain Boys, under Col. Seth Warner, appeared at the same time, and the British were again defeated and compelled to retreat.

Miss Jane McCrea of Fort Edwards was engaged to marry Lt. David Jones, an officer of Burgoyne army. She left her home by stealth and paid a direful penalty. The Indian, whom she accompanied and whom Jones had sent, met in the woods a second pary, whom he had unwisely dispatched to aid the first. They quarreled; each determined to conduct the lady to their employer. The first, finding the second to succeed, tied her to a tree and tomahawked her to death to prevent the other from receiving the barrel of rum promised in payment. This tragic affair excited the minds of the people against the British who had let loose the savages upon the land. A general rising led to five thousand reinforcements for the Americans.[49]

Burgoyne crossed the Hudson on the twelfth and encamped at Saratoga, about three miles from the American army. A bloody battle occurred at Stilhvater on the nineteenth. Both sides claimed victory. Skirmishes broke out till, on October 7, a general battle was fought at Saratoga. The Americans made the attack. The battle was fierce and desperate. The British gave way in fifty minutes. That short time decided great events. The loss was severe in killed and wounded on both sides. Arnold had greatly distinguished himself and was severely wounded.

This was Arnold's last battle for his still beloved country, yet no tidings of his bravery came to Congress from the envious Horatio Gates. The disagreement between the two arose from Gates receiving no credit while Arnold received all the credit for the Stillwater success. Gates crowned his injustice by taking away Arnold's division. Arnold's nature was too proud to bear this. How many hours of despair would have been avoided if Arnold had learned in childhood to brook an insult?[50]

Burgoyne made effort to retreat, but Fort Edward was already in the hands of the Americans; he was hemmed in by a foe whose army was constantly increasing and now amounted to four times his own numbers. Still Burgoyne was too proud to submit to his fate and yield all his bright visions of future fame and glory at once. He resisted until the last moment, his bloodlines the same as those who now waited for victory, hope after hope fading, until worn out and weary he agreed, after much consultation, upon an honorable surrender of the relics of his once splendid army of ten thousand men. It was stipulated that on the seventeenth, they were to march out of their camp with the honors of war, to the place assigned, where their arms and artillery were to he piled at the command of their own officers. That a passage should be allowed them to Great Britain, on condition of their not serving again during the war.

The whole number of the British, 5,791 men, surrendered. Every possible courtesy was shown to the officers, and our soldiers were not allowed to witness the surrender. We here see one of the most unexpected reverses of fortune, as ordained by divine Providence. The proud, presuming foe, the haughty commander who threatened to lay waste to our cities and expose our helpless women to the merciless Hessians and savages, who said his army would not retreat, was at last obliged to sue for terms of surrender to the very people he had treated with sovereign contempt. With the long and loud huzza of victory from an oppressed people arose another cry over the land, of praise to Him who limits the extent of human power and decrees in wisdom the destinies of nations. Those who embrace terror will submit to those terrorized.

Gen. Schuyler, notwithstanding Burgoyne had in wantonness ordered his splendid countryseat near Saratoga to be destroyed, opened his old family to the captive officers. Burgoyne learned a lesson on the beauty of forgiveness and could not forbear saying to Gen. Schuyler, "You show me great kindness, sir, though I have done you much injury." To which the noble-hearted Schuyler replied, "That was the fate of war, think no more of it."[51]

On hearing of the defeat of Burgoyne, the British garrison at Ticonderoga returned to Canada; not a foe remained in the northern section of the Union. Sir Henry Clinton returned to New York having first barbarously burned Esopus (Kingston).

Gen. Howe, intent on the capture of Philadelphia, left Sandy Hook on July 23 and sailed up the Chesapeake with eighteen thousand troops, disembarking at the head of the bay. Washington crossed the Delaware and marched to oppose them. Approaching the enemy, he encamped on the rising grounds that extend from Chad's Ford and there, the shallow stream of the Brandywine being between. them, he awaited an attack from the British commander.

Early morning the hostile *army* commenced the assault. Washington, on bad intelligence, lost the battle (Gen. Green here distinguished himself, as did the brave Polander, Casimir Pulaski). General La Fayette, endeavoring to return to face again the enemy, received a wound in the leg.

> When *in his* old age, our beloved America, for which he had shed blood and had helped win her freedom conveyed him, and honored guest, on his return to France aboard the new warship, the Brandywine named after his most famous battle for liberty.[52]

Congress, finding their presence insecure in Philadelphia, adjourned to Lancaster, to which place the archives and magazines were removed. Cornwallis entered the American capital, while Howe took post at Germantown. The American army encamped at Skippack creek. Washington left his camp on the evening of Oct 4 and at dawn succeeded in giving the British a complete slap. They at first retreated, but then a thick fog rolled in and confusion ensued. The Americans retreated.

Congress had made it death to any citizen who provided food to the enemy, and such was the spirit of the people; Howe now found his army in danger of starvation. To prevent this he had to open the navigation of the Delaware, which was blocked by debris of battles.

They attacked Fort Mercer and were repulsed, then sent in such a force the Americans retreated. The British fleet then passed up the Delaware to Philadelphia, burning much of the American shipping and capturing the remainder.

Washington now retired to winter quarters at Valley Forge. The huts for the camp were not completed when the magazines were found to contain scarcely a single day's provision. As for clothing, they were almost destitute to nakedness. Barefooted on the frozen ground-their feet cut by the ice-they left their tracks in blood. A few only had a blanket at night. Numbed by cold, a cold damp ground was their bed. Diseases attacked, and the hospitals were replenished as soon as the dead were carried out. Congress had printed up paper money without gold or silver to actually pay the notes. People began to doubt it would ever be redeemed, and if they had articles to sell they would not accept the paper money for their goods. The country was so poor, the people had nothing left to give, and the consequence was that they could not provide either food or clothes for the army.

Pay for the officers was not sufficient to sustain life; those spending their own fortunes and those who had not fortune were in a state of actual suffering. Amidst the grief and care, to which the commander was subjected, a cabal was stirred up to prejudice the minds of the people against him and thus to get his office for Gen. Gates. The most active of the plot was Gen. Thomas Conway. Even Congress so far gave way to appoint this man inspector-general. Washington, in the calmness of his righteous mind, turned not aside from his public duties to notice his private enemies. The people took his part and the army was so indignant that, at length, all who had been engaged in the plot, whatever had been their former, were not afraid of their resentment and kept out of the way. Conway's office was given to Baron Wilhelm Steuben, a Prussian officer.[53]

A law was passed, the object of which was to make the officers to remain in the army. It allowed them half-pay for seven years after the close of the war. The Americans were successful in the depredations their swift sailing privateers made upon the British commerce. With these they boldly scoured every sea, even those about the British Islands. Since 1776 they had captured five hundred of the British vessels. Early in the season, Sir Henry Clinton arrived in Philadelphia to supersede Sir William Howe.

The news of the capture of Burgoyne caused a deep sensation in Europe. The English people were astonished and afflicted. The French acknowledge the independence of the United States of America. A treaty of alliance was made on February 6, by which it was stipulated that France and the United States should make common cause; and that neither party should make either peace or truce with England without the consent of the other; and neither party lay down their arms, till the independence of the United States was secured. The American commissioners Franklin, Deane, and Lee were received at the court of France as the representatives of a sister nation. M. Gerard was appointed minister to the United States. Dr Franklin, still in France, was the following September made capitol minister plenipotentiary. Intelligence was brought that other European powers were favorably inclined to the Republican cause.

After the country had been deluged with the blood of its inhabitants, and after innumerable acts of violence and tyranny, the British meanly offered to give them what they asked for in humble terms. "No!" America said with one voice. "Independence now and independence forever." Never would they return to the mother country as a subject. They were firm in this resolve to the last. They had pledged their lives, their fortunes, and their sacred honors to the cause of American independence. They felt the justice of their cause and had a strong confidence in the overruling providence of God, and though deficient in many things necessary to *carry* on the war, and apparently incompetent for the contest, they determined to press onward.

The British now sent over three men, Carlisle, Eden, and Johnstone, under pretense of treating for peace, but in reality to plot secretly against the government established in the United States and to draw off influential individuals, by direct bribery, and the promises of wealth and titles for the future. Johnstone offered to General Joseph Reed, if he would aid the royal cause, ten thousand pieces of sterling and any office in the colonies within the king's gift.

"I am not," said General Reed, "worth purchasing; but such as I am, the king of England is not rich enough to buy me."[54]

In some instances, Johnstone offered the bribes in written letter, which the indignant patriots brought forward these letters, which contained the evidence of his base intrigues, and Congress indignantly forbade all further communication.

I think a little tar and feathers would have sent a better message. Of course, I am from the middle-class.

The pride of the British nation had been greatly humbled by the defeat of its favorite general, and the ministry received the loudest censures from the party that had opposed the war. They had been foiled in their attempt at negotiations and bribery and were at a loss what new method to adopt.

The ratification of the treaty of alliance warned them that French troops would soon join heart and hand with Americans. Deeming Philadelphia a disadvantageous position, the British army, on June 18, evacuated the city and, marching through New Jersey, now directed their course to New York. Gen. Howe had resigned, Sir Henry Clinton was appointed commander, and on him devolved the execution of these orders.

Howe immediately set about the movement in the most secret manner, but the plan was uncovered by the troops stationed at Valley Forge. Washington dispatched Lafayette with two thousand men to watch the enemy and guard the country against their marauding parties. He took post on Barren Hill, midway between Valley Forge and Philadelphia, about nine miles from either place.

A spy brought information of his movement to Sir Henry Clinton. He immediately sent out a superior force against Lafayette to surprise him and by cutting off his retreat, forced him to surrender. Through negligence of one of Lafayette's piquet guards, he was nearly surrounded at night. At sunrise, a spectacle that was sufficient to appall an older heart than Lafayette's met his gaze the British troops strongly guarding one of the fords of that river, while a large detachment was readying to descend upon him

Cool and collected, Lafayette hesitated not a moment. He dared not attack so large a body, but he would not surrender. He had recourse to a plan, which gave him great credit. Forming his little band in forms of columns, which only extended beyond the woods, the British were led to suppose that the whole army was advancing against them and halted to give battle. In the mean time, beneath the very hill on which the British were posted, Lafayette was silently passing on his way, when at last, to the utter surprise of the enemy, the heads of the columns retreated with speed, and the whole detachment reached Valley Forge. Washington embraced his youthful friend; the army received him with joyful shouts. The retreat at Barren Hill has always been regarded as a most skillful achievement.

The number of troops at Valley Forge in May of that year was about eleven thousand, and the whole American force did not exceed fifteen thousand. The British force amounted to thirty thousand with four thousand more in Rhode Island.

On June 28, the two armies were warmly engaged at Monmouth. The action was conducted with great skill on both sides. This battle was fought on the Sabbath day, and the engagement was fierce. All day long they fought on the plains of Monmouth, the sun pouring down rays of intense heat, the thermometer being ninety-six degrees. Many of the soldiers died from the heat, and the cry for water was more awful than the moans of the wounded. An unfortunate retreat permitted by Gen. Lee nearly deranged the plan of operation, and but for the singular bravery of General Washington, who commanded the troops in person, the battle would have been lost.

When word came to Washington that Lee was in full retreat, the expression of his usually placid face is said to have been dreadful. With a burst of indignation, he sprang on his horse, and the cloud of dust alone told his route.

"Long live Washington!" the troops shouted as he galloped furiously on until, reining up in Lee's presence, he demanded of him in tones of severity, "Whence arose the disorder and confusion?"

Rebuke from Washington was terrible to anyone, but galling to the extreme to Lee. Not a moment was to be lost. Commands were given in quick succession and promptly obeyed.

Order once more was restored when Washington again rode up to Lee and in token of forgiveness, exclaimed, "Will you, sir, command in that place!" he said, pointing to the front, exposed to the rapid fire of the British.

Lee sullenly replied. "Yes."

"I expect you to check the enemy immediately!" shouted Washington.

"Your orders?" replied Lee, stung with mortification. "Shall be obeyed. I shall not be the first to leave the field."[55]

Lee, incapable of brooking even an implied indignity, addressed two letters to the commander-in-chief, couched in disrespectful language and with an air of defiance solicited a trial for his conduct. He was immediately put under arrest, charged with disobedience of orders, misbehavior before the enemy, and *disrespect of the commander-in-chief.* He was found guilty of all charges and was sentenced to suspension from any command of the American army for one year. From that moment, his attacks on the character of Washington were more virulent and open and his language at all times scurrilous and profane. He lived a wretched life, secluded from society in a hovel without glass windows or plastering, until the autumn of 1782 when he took lodgings in a common tavern in Philadelphia. He was soon seized with a violent disease, which speedily terminated his life on October 2, 1782. He was an atheist in principle and hostile to every attribute of the Deity. In his will he requested not to be buried in any church or churchyard or within a mile of any Presbyterian or Anabaptist meetinghouse. What a contrast between such a deathbed scene and that of a Christian.[56]

(For those who have bad-mouthed my President, I agree, we should adhere to our Founders' thoughts and actions. Line them up boys for prosecution!")

A deadly fire was poured on them, and nobly they stood their ground. Alexander Hamilton was exposed to the hottest fire and fearing lest Lee might again shrink under the heavy onset, exclaimed, "I will stay with you-I will die with you-let us all die rather than retreat!"

The batteries of Knox and Stirling were like sheets of flame, and everything betokened the energy with which the battle was fought. Night only put an end to the incessant firing, and as the thunder of the guns faded away, both armies, exhausted under the burning sun, lay down upon the ground. The stillness of that awful Sabbath evening was broken by piteous cries for water and groans of dying. The wearied Americans slept soundly, for at dawn of day they perceived the British had deserted their camp and were beyond their reach. The Americans lost eight officers and sixty-one privates, while the British lost 350 men in battle, fifty-nine more on the retreat from heat, one thousand deserted, and one hundred were taken prisoner. The victory was celebrated with rejoicing throughout the United States, and Congress passed a vote of thanks to General Washington and his army for their bravery.

The French fleet, tall ships in full billowing sail, commanded by Count d'Eataing, arrived and joined forces with the American army; an Indian uprising was occurring on the western frontier but was quelled by the intrepid Col. George Rogers Clarke who put an end to the outrages.

There is not a spot on our guilty earth un-cursed by evil, including the lonely and sequestered vale of Wyoming and the scene of horror it witnessed.

Settled by pious people many years before the Revolution, the call to arms had their sons joining the cause. Party split arose, and the inhabitants were divided into Whigs and Tories, with the Tories in the majority. Taking advantage of the absence of the sons, they resolved on one of the blackest acts recorded. Joining to their number several hundred Indians, anxious to witness the annihilation of the whites increasing their forces to about 1,600 they started on their demoniacal errand.

The blue skies shined, but the anxious faces and tearful eyes of the women and the hurried step and quickened speech masked the feeling of dread that danger was approaching and there was little they could do to stop it.

Their fears were somewhat calmed by Col. John Butler, Tory commander, who claimed he wanted to parley, and the men of the camp went out to meet them. Instantly the work of murder commenced, and nearly every man was butchered in the most awful manner.

The women fled to the fort, and Col. Dennison, who was left in command of the remaining men, waited in shock. Soon the horrid band came with yells and imprecations to the fort, and to make their errand known, they threw the bleeding scalps of the 196 heads of their loved ones into the fort. Feeling resistance to be in vain, several were sent out to inquire the terms of surrender, to which Butler replied, "The Hatchet!" A few moments completed the horrid act. The men were murdered; the women with their babies were locked in the houses and fort and burned alive. Similar acts of atrocity took place at Cherry Valley in New York and Tappan, but I forbear: the story of such inhumanity sickens my heart. Terrorists are not new, and once they were neighbors with the same prophet.[57]

In November, Sir Henry Clinton dispatched Col. Campbell with about two thousand troops to commence operations against Georgia, then one of the weakest States. The American forces under the command of their General Robert Howe were inadequate to resist the enemy. They fought bravely but were overcome, and after a short contest the capital surrendered and the whole of Georgia came under British possession. This was the only State in the Union in which a legislative body assembled under the authority of Great Britain after the Declaration of Independence. 1778 closed with Washington retiring to winter quarters near Middle-Brook in New Jersey.[58]

Never had the finances of the country been in so low a state, as in the beginning of 1779.

Never had party spirit and private jealousies been more rife in Congress than at this moment. (Wish I could show them 2020.) A gloomy prospect was presented to the American patriot. Here, again, the peculiar virtues and talents of Washington were exhibited in their brightest light. Attacked by misrepresentations and angry speeches and loaded with a weight of troubles both in camp and out, still hoping and confiding in the arm of Providence, onward he went in the path of duty, the great and good man imitating the meek and lowly One, who, when He was reviled, reviled nothing back.

Washington spent some time in Philadelphia with Congress, maturing a plan for the campaign. It was concluded to hold the army entirely on the defensive, with the exception of visiting with condign punishment on the Tories and Indians who had committed such merciless ravages the preceding year. This defensive plan was necessary, as the treasury was exhausted. Efforts to secure loans in Europe had only obtained small sums.

Throughout this year the British in the North thrived on depredation and butchery. For this purpose an expedition was fitted out of New York against Virginia, in which private and public property was destroyed, and the most ferocious cruelty everywhere marked their path. In twenty-one days, Portsmouth and Norfolk were seized, 127 vessels were taken or burned, and $2.5 million worth of property was destroyed. It was an expedition only worthy of Goths, undertaken merely for plunder.

A similar expedition was made against Connecticut, under Gov. Tyron. He was chosen by Gen. Clinton to commit acts of brutality. No act was too vile for him to perform, no place too sacred to desecrate. New Haven, Fairfield, and Norwalk were visited and exhibited fearful scenes of plunder, conflagration, and distress. Before applying the torch, the soldiers were allowed to plunder the homes and steal whatever they chose. After these terrorists left, females, frantic, compromised, and starving, were found wandering in swamps where they had fled for safety.[59]

Washington could do little to protect these places. Dividing the small force would risk the whole to be destroyed, and until he had an army to cover the whole country, he deemed it prudent to risk no more than was consistent with the general welfare.

About this time Gen. Putnam performed his celebrated feat of riding down the stone stairs at Horse Neck. Gov. Tyron who had 1,500 men and stopped the advance of the enemy until he saw the infantry and cavalry preparing for a charge attacked him with 150 men. Putnam instantly ordered his men to a neighboring swamp and, plunging his rowels in his steed, rode down the precipice to the utter consternation and chagrin of the British dragoons. A shower of balls was poured upon him; he remained unharmed, though one pierced his hat. After procuring reinforcement, he faced about and pursued Gov. Tryon, taking fifty prisoners.[60]

The taking of Stony Point was a memorable feat of 1779. Washington committed this hazardous enterprise to the gallant Wayne. On the evening of July 16, after marching fourteen miles over lofty heights with his band of zoo, he approached the fort. An advance party of twenty men attacked the double palisade of the fort.

Wayne shouted to his men, "On to the fort, my brave men!"

At last the heavy axes of the advance party forced the way, and a sound of joy sounded through the air. At this moment their gallant leader fell wounded in the head.

Although wounded he said to his men, "March on and carry me to the fort. I will die at the head of my column."

They lifted him and bore him forward until the center of the fort was reached and both parties met. The fort and stores fell into American hands.

The brave and scrupulous were in the observance of the laws of humanity toward a conquered foe. Our honest soldiers abstained from pillage or disorder and disdained to take the lives of those who asked quarter; thus showing as was said to Wayne, *'Bravery, humanity, and magnanimity are the national virtues of the Americans.*[61]

While these events were transpiring in the North, scenes of equal interest were enacted in Georgia and South Carolina. The enemy was encouraged by hope of speedy victory, as the country was weak through scanty population, numerous Negroes, and Tories.

Gen. Lincoln was dispatched to collect the army after it was scattered after the battle of Savannah in December 1778 and to defend the inhabitants as much as possible from the marauding attacks of the British and the Tories. Many of these were men of infamous character, more solicitous for booty and blood than for the interest of the king. They had been reinforced by troops from Florida, and Prevost received the chief command of the Southern British army, replacing Campbell who returned to England.

The first objective of the British was to get possession of Port Royal in South Carolina, but they were met by Col Moultrie and repulsed with great loss.

A bold attempt was executed to regain Georgia; Gen. Ash pushed them as far as Briar Creek but was fallen upon from the rear by Prevost, losing a forth of his army, and the British held Georgia. Great apprehensions were now entertained for the safety of the adjacent States, and the brave Carolinians, defeated but not discouraged, gathered around the standard of Lincoln. John Rutledge, a man beloved and well known in that region, was elected Governor and invested with dictatorial powers.

The condition of the southern States claimed the immediate attention of Congress, as Lincoln's army consisted of a few hundred continentals and a few inexperienced militias; and many of these were impatient to return to their homes. Washington sent a part of his own small band and solicited D'Estaing, who was engaged in operations against the British in the West Indies, to proceed immediately to the southern States, to engage in the fall campaign.

D'Estaing accepted the invitation and in September appeared off the coast of Georgia to the great surprise of the British; D'Estaing captured three frigates and a fifty-gun ship. The British concentrated on Savannah and prepared for its defense. D'Estaing demanded surrender of the city, which Prevost refused. Immediately thirty-seven cannon and nine mortars, accompanied by sixteen heavy guns from the fleet, opened fire. In defiance, one hundred cannon sounded from the garrison. The exchange roared day and night for five days, with no break or compromise. The suffering of the inhabitants was immense.

At last D'Estaing and Lincoln determined on an assault leading on their armies, three columns of the French and one of the Americans. D'Estaing was wounded. The contest wore on, and two hundred horsemen charged with Pulaski at their head-but he was mortally wounded. Then came the gallant Laurens, regardless of the danger. He found his brave band routed and confused. In desperation he flung away his sword, and with his noble soul wringing in despair, stretched forth his hands and prayed for death.

Near him was the beloved of all who knew him; the simple-hearted, self-denying Jasper, grasping in death the standard presented to his regiment at Fort Moultrie.

The British sustained slight losses, but stretched upon the field were more than one thousand Frenchmen and Americans. D'Estaing was anxious to embark to Europe, and Lincoln was obliged to return to South Carolina.

> (The French fleet encountered severe storms on its return and arrived at Brest in a very shattered condition. D'Estaing was one of the victims of the guillotine during the French Revolution.)

During the summer of that year, Gen. Sullivan was successful in his expedition against the Indians and Tories under the command of Brandt, Butler, and others who were implicated in the massacre at Wyoming. He boldly pursued them to the heart of their country, burned forty Indian villages, destroyed corn stores, and every vestige of their industry. After two months he returned to Pennsylvania, having lost only forty men. The Indians were intimidated by this severe chastisement, and the frontier settlements enjoyed repose for a time.

This year was signalized by the victories achieved by our infant Navy, which was under the command of Paul Jones. The French government aided our commissioners in fitting out a squadron of three frigates and two smaller vessels, with Jones commanding. After capturing some vessels off the coast of Scotland, he fell in with a Baltic merchant fleet of forty-one sail, under convoy of the British frigate Serapis and the Countess Scarborough. The convoy immediately separated, but the two frigates advanced to battle with flowing sheets. The England coast, off Flamborough, was covered with spectators.

At the close of this September day, the hostile vessels commenced to fire. With the British having superior guns, Jones ordered his ship to be lashed to that of the enemy. The action then became terrific, the muzzles of the enemy guns touching theirs and the gunners, ramming their cartridges, often thrust their ramrods into the enemy's ports. Pearson, the British commander tried to separate the vessels without results. The details of this battle surpass any kind recorded in naval warfare. The Bon Homme Richard of Jones was old and rotten and, by the incessant firing had become almost unmanageable, and soon, only three guns were effective.

Then Jones started assailing the enemy with grenades, which set fire to the Serapis in several places. In the midst of the uproar, a cry was heard. The Bon Homme Richard was sinking, and an awful accident occurred when another vessel of Paul's squadron mistakenly shot a broadside through the sinking ship's side, which released one hundred English prisoners. Capt. Pearson hailed to know if colors were struck, which Paul answered by ordering the prisoners to the pumps or drown. It is beyond power to describe this frightful scene during the four hours before his beloved lady sank, carrying three hundred victims with her. The Separis, at length as the fire rolled around her mast, stuck her colors, and Jones was the conqueror. Over the following three months, Jones took more than a quarter of a million dollars worth of prizes and Louis XVI awarded him the Order of Merit and Congress gave him a vote of thanks and presented him with a gold medal to commemorate the victory.[62]

This campaign terminated in gloom. The Americans had a feeble army reduced numbers and an exhausted treasury, while Great Britain was redoubling her energies, having boundless resources at his command. Parliament agreed to send one hundred twenty thousand men to America and voted 50 million for the support of the war. Washington did not have such resources at his command he saw, with anguish, a discontented, starving army on the verge of mutiny, Congress convulsed and weakened by dissensions, an inefficient ally in France, and in bitterness and grief he declared, "Friends and foes were combining to pull down the fabric they had been raising at the expense of so much time, blood, and treasure." So much will be lost if we allow failure to prevail.[63]

Please forgive my tears as I write these words. The Southern citizens faced untold misery and pain as evil men sought to conquer these brave patriots and squash Liberty into submission.

Disaffection to the American cause was daily increasing in the South, while the adherents to the crown were becoming more numerous. The successive defeats of the Americans during a protracted war and the numerous miseries accompanying such a state of affairs made the people long for peace. Savannah was in the hands of the British troops; Sir Henry Clinton, taking advantage of the departure of the French fleet, resolved to gain possession of the capital of South Carolina. Leaving the command of the royal army to Gen. Knyphauscn, he sailed from New York on December 26, 1779, with eight thousand troops and a large amount of military stores.

Clinton had not gotten far when a violent storm arose and drove them far off course. The vessel carrying the heavy ordnance was lost, and nearly all the cavalry horses and most of the artillery perished. They landed among the Tory population, began repairs, and prepared for the siege on Charleston.

Gen. Lincoln was at Charleston doing everything possible to prepare for a bold defense. He had only a small band amounting to three thousand effective men and some armed citizens to check the approach of nine thousand veteran troops.

On April 9, Clinton sent a summons to General Lincoln to surrender, which he promptly refused, and the siege commenced, continuing for ten days, when again he summoned for surrender. After a vain and desperate struggle, day after day and night after night, amid the most alarming discouragements, shut up by sea and of all provisions, save some rice, Lincoln, at last, listened to the entreaties of the distressed inhabitants and capitulated.

On May 12, his entire army laid down their arms, and South Carolina was given over to the exulting troops of a rapacious and sanguinary foe. There was scarcely a soldier who was not either in arms for the crown or a prisoner on parole. The number that surrendered was about six thousand, including one thousand American and French seamen. The loss numbered Americans with 254 killed or wounded and the British with 268 dead.

Clinton immediately endeavored to gain the entire possession of Georgia and dispatched three detachments to seize important posts. Georgetown and Ninety-Six were captured; the country bordering on the Santee was scoured, while the bloodthirsty Tarleton spread terror and death wherever he passed. When the helpless and dying sued for quarter, begging for mercy from this terror that overwhelmed them, it was refused, and whole bands of men who after fighting bravely were forced to surrender then barbarously murdered. Feeling satisfied he had made Liberty bleed profusely, Clinton embarked for New York, leaving Cornwallis with an army of four thousand men to complete the death of liberty in the South. In a short time the terms of the treaty, signed at surrender, were openly and grossly violated, and the people, who under honest and kind treatment would have quietly obeyed, arose indignantly at such treachery. Against their agreement, they were about to compel them to fight in their armies. "If we must fight, it will be for America and our friends, not for

England and strangers," defiantly exclaimed the people of America's capital southern colonies.

The women of Carolina refused their captors presence at every scene of gaiety. Like the daughters of captured Zion, they would not amuse or entertain them. But at every hazard they honored with their attention the brave defenders of their country. Sisters encouraged brothers, wives embraced husbands, the mothers praised their sons, and their parting advice was, "Prefer prisons to infamy, and death to servitude."

In every part of the nation, that fire of patriotism that had burned so brightly in the beginning of the Revolution was rekindled. The Militia and men of the capital came forward with alacrity. The women, with Martha Washington at their head, formed an industrious society to make clothing for the soldiers. All seemed ready to contribute in such ways that they could for the cause.

Cornwallis had issued a proclamation, stating that whoever would not take an active part in securing his majesty's government should be treated as rebels. Many suffered for a time, but, his cruelty becoming more insufferable, they formed themselves in small bands for partisan warfare. These bands spread desolation among the Tories. Among the leaders of these bands, and foremost for bravery and integrity of purpose, were Marion and Sumter. Many a tale is recorded of boldness of these noble men, who, regardless of personal emolument, thought only of their country and liberty for their children.

A British officer had been sent from Georgetown to negotiate an exchange of prisoners and was taken to Gen. Marion's tent. An interesting interview took place, during which the officer partook with Marion of a humble dinner of roasted sweet potatoes. He was so affected by Marion's sentiments and ardent love for liberty, that on his return he resigned his commission and retired from the service, declaring it was useless to fight against such men. He had little dreamed of the privations of our people until he saw an American general and his officers working without pay, almost without clothes, dining on roots, and drinking nothing but water and all these privations endured for Liberty.[64]

These bands of patriots were without pay; they wore no uniform and depended from day to day on chance for subsistence. Often they were destitute of ammunition and were obliged to watch as their companions shot down an enemy, when they would instantly seize their musket and cartridges. Sawmills furnished them broadswords, and the patriot women, with their own hands, melted down their pewter dishes to make bullets. At night, the cold earth was their resting place, but frequently they marched through the darkness to stay warm.

France, determined to assist the Americans and persuaded by Lafayette, dispatched in July, with a squad of seven sail of the line, twenty frigates and armed vessels, plus six thousand men under the command of Count de Rochambeau. But before they had time to act, they were stopped by a blockade at Rhode Island by Adm. Arbuthnot.

This was a deep disappointment for the Americans, but a deeper one was in store for them. They could brave all the horrors of war, the rigors of winter, scantily clad and nearly starved endure absence from home and all its endearments, with few murmurs and with manly hearts but, a shudder of indignation and a heart sickness overcame them when the treason of Arnold was brought to light.

Benedict Arnold, a traitor! Arnold, who had been loaded with the praises of a grateful country, a traitor? Saratoga's bloody field and many others came to remembrance, and with hearts aching with mingled pity and shame, they again in consternation asked, "Is Arnold a traitor?" He had been among the first to widen the breach between the mother country and the colonies. Arnold, with a maimed body, wounded in fighting valiantly for liberty, a traitor! From one end of the Union to the other, the news flew like lightning; even little children ran with trembling steps and whitened lips, borrowing anxiety *from* their parents, lisping, *Benedict Arnold a traitor!*

As a warning to youth, we dwell on this painful story because we cannot forget all that he bravely suffered in the early struggles of our nation.

A TRAITORS STORY

After the evacuation of Philadelphia by the British in 1778, Arnold was stationed there as military governor; his wounds at Saratoga for a time prevented his engaging in active duty. While in Philadelphia he selected a wife from one of the Tory families. His wife was instrumental in weakening his attachment to his country. He hired a splendid mansion, furnished it in a sumptuous style, and, having expended most of his private fortune in the war, he found difficulty in meeting his expenses. Rather than retrench his extravagances, he resorted to dishonest means to procure money, and by a system of fraud and deceit succeeded in appropriating public treasure to his private use. At length, Washington, who was ever indulgent and forgiving to Arnold, arraigned him before a court-martial and reprimanded with all possible delicacy.

But he had been determined to retrieve his fortunes and gratify his passion for revenge under wrongs inflicted, and in an evil hour, he consented to barter away the liberties for which he had so nobly fought. He was too proud to become a deserter, and gold he thought he must have in some way.

At last, he opened a correspondence with Sir Henry Clinton, and speedily after that the infamous work proceeded. He had procured from Washington the command of the fortress at West Point (in the vaults laid the ammunition for its own defense and the stock of powder for the whole army), which for its strength had been called the Gibraltar of America. It was more important than any other post, as it commanded the whole extent of the country from New York to Canada and secured a communication between the eastern and southern States. For £ 30,000 sterling *(thirty pieces off silver sold out another, once, long ago)* and the rank of brigadier-general in the British army," Arnold, at last, agreed to betray his country and place West Point in Sir Henry Clinton's hands.

Taking advantage of the absence of the vigilant Washington, who had gone to Harford to meet Count Rochambeau, he resolved to finish quickly the foul deed, and for that purpose held a conference with Major John Andre (Andre was a warm friend of Arnold's wife), the adjutant-general of the British army. All *of* Arnold's plans were laid before Andre September 21, 1780, and it was agreed he would surrender the fort. Arnold would signal the transports, and they were to sail up the Hudson and land their troops and capture West Point. This one act would divide America and give a superior advantage to the British to squash the revolt and end America's quest for independence. All American children are familiar with the story, but perhaps they have not recognized the hand of Providence in thwarting the traitor's plan.

Sir Henry Clinton had enjoined it on Andre not to leave the sloop-of-war Vulture, on account of the firing from an American vessel, which had moved down the river; then in the stubborn refusal of the man who brought him ashore, to take him back the next day—his unaccountable determination to change his route after parting with his guide—his confusion and loss of presence of mind when arrested on the road by three Americans, John Paulding, David Williams, and Isaac Van Wert are miraculous links in a chain of Providential events, in which an imposing hand is plainly visible. The three patriots found Arnold's dispatches and plans in Andre's boot. He offered them his horse, watch, purse, and large rewards from the British government if they would let him go. Although they were poor men, they could not be bribed, declaring, *"No sum would convince them to sell out their America!"*

Andre was examined before a court and found guilty of being a spy, punishable by death. Washington and his officers would have gladly saved his life, but necessity required rigorous enforcement of the punishment. Andre wrote a letter that he might be shot, but this could not be granted according to the strict rules of war. His request was denied, and on October 2, 1780, he was hung as a spy. The

British and the Americans universally lamented Andre; the spot of his suffering and interment was consecrated by thousands of tears.[65]

(The American spy Hale, who gave his life in service to his country, seems to have been forgotten by his countrymen. I remember his last words, "I lament I have but one life to lose for my country!" To the memory of Hale, not a stone has been erected, nor an inscription to preserve his ashes from insult written. Note: America does remember her heroes. A statue of Hale was erected in New York City Hall Park in 1890; his image appeared on U.S. postage stamps in 1925 and 1929, and in 1985 he was designated as a Connecticut state hero.)

His body was never found. No picture of him exists, and sadly he was hung sometime in the first part of September 1776.

GLOOM AND DOOM-1781

At no period during the war were the prospects of the Americans so gloomy than at the commencement of 1781. On the first of January 1, 300 Pennsylvania troops, rendered desperate by their sugaring and contending they were detained beyond their time of service, declared their intentions to march in a body to Philadelphia and demand redress for all their grievances. They mutinied because their sufferings were intolerable, and to show they were still firm friends to their country, they cheerfully returned to duty when their grievances were only in part redressed. Sir Henry Clinton offered them remuneration if they would join his forces, but they indignantly scorned his offers and delivered over the emissaries sent from his camp to Wayne, who executed them as spies.

A similar mutiny was undertaken in New jersey troops, and as this state of things became alarming, Washington determined to punish them severely, as a warning to others. Two of the ringleaders were shot by the guiltiest of the mutineers. This was a most painful task; being culprits themselves, they were greatly distressed, and when ordered to load, many of them shed tears. It was important the spirit of revolt should be effectually repressed, or the ruin of the army was inevitable.

Congress now felt that the sufferings of the troops were pitiable, and unprecedented efforts were made to raise money and supply the needs of the army. Taxes were imposed and cheerfully paid by the citizens to provide for their defenders. A commissioner was sent to Europe to negotiate loans of money; large amounts of gold and silver were acquired by the beneficial trade with the Spanish West India Islands.

During that year a charter from Congress, under the supervision of Robert Morris, established the Bank of North America. To this distinguished patriot, the *army* was greatly indebted, for he used his own ample private fortune and his personal credit, without hesitation, to sustain the government. The issuing of paper money was discontinued. Two hundred million paper dollars were made redeemable by 5 million in silver, and this with every other arrangement was submitted to without murmur, in hope of a happier future.

The British enlarged their plan of operations and hostilities raged, not only around their headquarters at New York, but in Georgia, North and South Carolina, Virginia, and Connecticut. In the latter places, the traitor Arnold became notorious for his plundering achievements as an incendiary and robber. Even in his native state, in the very spot of his boyhood's home, he rested not in his work of destruction.

The British, encouraged by their good fortunes in the reduction of Savannah and Charleston, determined to advance into North Carolina. After the unfortunate battle of Camden, Congress appointed Gen. Greene as the successor to Gen. Gates. Washington spoke in high terms of recommendation of Gen. Greene, but added, what can a general do without men, arms, clothes, provisions, or stores? The Southern army had been reduced to two thousand men, more than half militia. Although Gen. Greene's men were scantily clad, half-starved, and dispirited, destitute of arms and ammunition, the officers under his command were as brave men as ever followed a leader. Daniel Morgan, Charles Lee, Francis Marion, Thomas Sumter, and Col. William Washington banded together with a group to which the British army could furnish no parallel.

In order to procure subsistence for his army, as well as to distract and harass the enemy, Gen. Greene was constrained to divide his army by dispatching Gen. Morgan to the western frontier of South Carolina. Cornwallis had made preparations for invading North Carolina and was unwilling to leave an enemy in the rear. He sent Tarleton, at the head of 1,000 men, to dislodge him and "push him to the utmost. They met at Cowpens. On January 17, and after one of the severest conflicts witnessed in the war, Tarleton was defeated with the loss of three hundred men, along with five hundred prisoners, his artillery, and baggage. The defeat of Tarleton was mortifying to himself and a surprise to Cornwallis; the loss of the high infantry crippled his movements during the campaign.

The battle of Cowpens, it has been justly remarked, proved, in the end, nearly as disastrous to Cornwallis as Bennington was to Burgoyne.

Cornwallis now determined to take the field in person, and, by a vigorous exertion, he expected soon to subdue the whole country south of Virginia.

PROVIDENCE EMBRACES LIBERTY
1782 TO 1784

On January 19, having destroyed all his excess baggage and all the wagons, except a few for necessary purposes, he commenced his pursuit of Morgan, who had moved off to Virginia with his prisoners. He marched with such rapidity that he reached the Catawba the evening of the same day Morgan had crossed. Cornwallis, not doubting his ability to overtake the adversary, halted for the night; but before morning the rain fell in torrents, the river was impassable without boats, and these the Americans had carefully removed to the other side.

The swelling of the river was regarded as a gracious interposition of God, as by it, the enemy was delayed two days. During this time, Gen. Greene, hearing of Morgan's victory, and afterward of the rapid pursuit by Cornwallis, ordered the remainder of his troops to march to his relief, while he, himself, with only two or three attendants, after a ride of 150 miles, arrived in Morgan's camp on January

To understand the ground over which this retreat occurred, one looks at a map and finds three large rivers in the northwest part of North and South Carolina, with the most southern the Catawba. Greene and Morgan were across and approaching Yadkin, which they passed on Feb 2, partly by fording, part by boat, secured on the other side. Here again, it happened on the Yadkin, the swelling to prevent the enemy from crossing. This second interposition in their behalf inspired them with fresh enthusiasm in that cause which seemed to be the peculiar care of God.

Cornwallis still determined to pursue, but the Americans toiled on, day after day, night after night, without a murmur, sleeping less than three hours out of twenty-four, and one meal a day. Pressing through a winter storm, most of them barefoot, with one blanket for four men, drenched by rains, chilled by river water, they dried their clothes by the heat of their own bodies.

Cornwallis continued his pursuit, hoping to overtake the Americans before they reached Virginia; but arriving at the Dan he found the Americans had already crossed, and a third time found the boats on the other side and the river unaffordable. So clear an interposition of Providence was this that the whole country regarded it as a special mark of favor to the American cause, and their hearts were cheered as they thought of the future. So firm was their belief in this that, although enduring severe conditions during the retreat of more than two hundred miles, not a single man deserted.

As soon as Greene had rested, he recrossed the Dan with an army of 4,500 men and, on March 15, reached Guilford Courthouse. It was a lonely spot, not another house being insight and a boundless forest on every side. On the day of Greene's arrival, Cornwallis attacked him. The battle raged for two hours, and all the advantages of victory were on the side of the Americans. They lost about four hundred in killed and wounded; the British nearly six hundred. Notwithstanding, Cornwallis claimed victory and he retreated, closely pursued by Greene.

Cornwallis avoided a battle and retreated to Wilmington, where he remained three weeks, then left the state and proceeded to Petersburg, in Virginia.

General Greene moved toward South Carolina to drive the British from their posts. Lord Rawdon attacked the Americans at Hobkirk's Hill, near Camden. At first, victory inclined toward the Americans, but at last they were compelled to retreat.

During April and May, several British posts fell into American hands. Marion and Lee invested Fort Washington on April 15. Though provided with muskets and rifles only, they were successful, and 114 men surrendered after a resistance of eight days. In rapid succession, post after post surrendered to small bodies of troops, led on by Marion, Sumter, Lee, and Pickens. On June 3, the British were confined to three posts: Ninety-six, Eutaw Springs, and Charleston.

Lord Rawdon resigned his command to Col. Stewart and in the beginning of September he took post at Eutaw Springs. Greene and Marion resolved to attack them at once, with the contest lasting over four hours, and the British were driven from the field, with losses of 1000 men killed, many wounded and taken prisoner. The Americans lost over five hundred; sixty of them were officers.. This battle was the last general action in South Carolina; the British, abandoning the open country, retreated to Charleston.

Cornwallis left North Carolina in April and arrived at Petersburg, in Virginia, on May 20. Having received several reinforcements and formed a junction with Arnold, the traitor, and Phillips, he flattered himself he should soon subjugate this section of the country. Lafayette had been dispatched with a small detachment from the main army to watch the motions of the British. They were unable to hinder the enemy from ravaging the countryside. (It was estimated that in the course of the invasion of Cornwallis, Arnold, Phillips, Leslie, and Collier about $15 million worth of property was destroyed. Thirty thousand Negroes were dragged from their homes, the young women compromised and brutalized. Estimated twenty-seven thousand died from smallpox or camp fever, and the survivors were forced on ships for sale in the West Indies.

Cornwallis soon after fortified himself at Yorktown on the south side of York River. Gloucester Point, opposite of Yorktown, was occupied by Tarleton. The British force in Virginia numbered seven thousand men.

Washington had made active preparations to form a junction with the French army, for the purpose of making a combined attack on New York. A letter was received from Count de Grasse, informing Washington he was leaving France with his whole fleet and about 3,200 land troops, for the Chesapeake. Washington proceeded to Virginia.

This movement met with the cordial cooperation of De Rochambeau, who was eager for defensive action. They took with them the whole French army and as many Americans that could be spared from the posts on the Hudson. A show of an intention to attack New York was still maintained, and so completely was Sir Henry Clinton deceived that is was not until the whole army had crossed Delaware that he suspected the real object of the Americans. Clinton hoped still to draw off part of their troops and perhaps cause Washington to return.

For this purpose he sent Arnold on a plundering expedition to Connecticut, but this did not affect the object. Washington and De Rochambeau pressed forward with the utmost alacrity At Chester, their spirits were greatly cheered by the intelligence of the arrival of Adm. de Grasse, who, with a large fleet, blockaded the Chesapeake and prevented the escape of the British by water. September 25, the combined troops reached Lafayette's headquarters at Williamsburg. (So complete was the discipline of the army that scarcely an apple or peach was taken without consent of the inhabitants). And on September 30, they marched in a body to invest Yorktown and Gloucester.

The allied army consisted of about sixteen thousand troops. As the British force did not amount to half that number, Cornwallis would probably have abandoned Yorktown before its investment, had he not confidently expected reinforcements from Clinton.

LIBERTY WON, BIRTH OF A NATION-1784 TO 1788

A close siege was commenced and carried on vigorously by the combined forces. During the siege, which lasted seventeen days, two redoubts were stormed simultaneously—one party of light infantry, headed by Lafayette and Col. Hamilton, the other by a detachment of French grenadiers under De Viomenil.

Finding his situation a desperate one, and further resistance of no avail, Cornwallis was obliged to surrender his whole army, amounting seven thousand, with six hundred killed; the Americans lost three hundred. On October 19, the articles of capitulation were signed and Gen. Benjamin Lincoln was selected by Washington to receive the sword of Cornwallis, on the same terms which the latter had, eighteen months before, received Lincoln's submission at Charleston. What goes around comes around.

About 12:00 p.m. the combined army was drawn up in two lines, extending more than a mile in length, the Americans on the right side of the road, with Washington at the head and the French on the left, headed by Count Rochambeau. A concourse of spectators assembled from the country, in numbers equal to the military. Every face beamed joy, but universal silence prevailed. About 2:00 p.m. the captive army advanced between the two lines with a slow step shouldered arms, and colors cased. Cornwallis, vexed and mortified, was unable to endure the humiliation of marching at the head of his garrison and made Gen. O'Hara his substitute. Tarleton's troops surrendered at the same time to the command of the French General, De Choise.[66]

The amount of artillery and military stores captured was very considerable—seventy-five brass and *169* iron cannon, *7,794* muskets, twenty-eight standards and 2,113 pounds of sterling taken from the military chest.

Lord Cornwallis and his officers, after their capitulation, received many civilities from Washington and other general officers, offering them food and lodging in their own homes for which they returned grateful acknowledgments.

The surrender of Cornwallis sent a thrill of joy through the country and was the most decisive event of the glorious war. The territory of the thirteen states was now restored to the jurisdiction of Congress, and the contest decided in favor of America. When Congress received the news of the brilliant success, the aged doorkeeper fainted from excess of joy. General Washington ordered divine service to be performed in the different brigades of the army, and the members of Congress marched in procession to church and there publicly offered up thanksgiving to God for the signal success of the American arms.

A proclamation was issued throughout the United States that December 13 be a day of thanksgiving and prayer. The many instances in which God's interposing hand was clearly seen were recounted. The public affirmed that "It was God, whose voice commands the winds, the seas, and the seasons, who formed a junction at the same time between a formidable fleet in the South and an army rushing from the North like an impetuous torrent. Who but He could so combine the circumstances which led to success?" It was the unparalleled perseverance of the armies of the United States through almost impossible suffering and discouragement for the space of eight long years that Washington declared was but a little short of a miracle.

It has been estimated that the loss of life during the war in the United States armies was not less than seventy thousand. It is unknown how many died on the prison ships of the enemy. No less than eleven thousand died on board the Jersey prison ship! These facts, with the whole story of our American Revolution, should be handed down to posterity; never forgotten the high price our fathers paid for freedom.

The people of Great Britain became clamorous for peace, and, at last, after much hesitation and discussion on the part of the British Government, they concluded to abandon the attempt to subjugate the United States.

Messrs. Jay, Franklin, Adams, and Laurens, our Commissioners, showed much firmness and wisdom, and through their negotiations, the primary articles of peace were settled at Paris on November 30, 1782, and on September 3, 1783, the Treaty of Paris was signed, ratified January 14, 1784, and by this treaty, Great Britain acknowledged the independence and sovereignty of the United States.

Thus the Americans obtained a high reward for their toils, and a sanctuary sacred to civil and religious liberty was opened in the western hemisphere.

The Patriot army was to be disbanded. Once more, fathers and husbands were free to return to their own firesides, but they went in extreme poverty. Many of them had not received compensation for five years. Anonymous letters were circulated tending to inflame their minds and induce them to insist on a forcible redress of grievances. Washington soothed them by kind words and promises, and in his farewell address appealed to the nobler sentiments of the heart. On November 3, 1783, still glowing with patriotism, they separated, resolved to endure all necessary privations.

On November 23, 1783, the British evacuated New York, this day celebrated for over a century as Evacuation Day.

On December 4, 1783, Washington, with a heart full of love and gratitude, bade his officer's adieu. It was a deeply affecting scene, and men who had braved the horrors of many a battle now, as they approached Washington, were melted to tears and incapable of utterance.

Washington then proceeded to Annapolis, the seat of Congress, to resign his commission as commander-in-chief of the armies of the United States. His parting words, "I consider it as an indispensable duty to close this last act of my official life by commending the interests of our dearest Country to the protection of Almighty God, and those who have the superintendence of them to His holy keeping."[67]

At the close of the war, the debt of the United States was estimated at $40 million, They were not able to pay the interest, and many incurred great losses. Congress had not the power to provide the means for discharging debts incurred during the war. During this disorganized state of the general government, attempts were made in some of the states to satisfy some of their creditors. Massachusetts attempted to affect this by levying a heavy tax and the people revolted against the unjust taxation. Shay's Rebellion, named after the leader Daniel Shay, had Massachusetts reversing this decision and calming the revolt.

In May 1787 deputies *from* each of the states, except Rhode Island, assembled at Philadelphia for the purpose of forming a new constitution. After four months' deliberation,, they presented the Constitution to the states, and finally, it was adopted.[68]

The blessings of civil and religious liberty are guaranteed to the people, and one of its chief excellences is that it contains a provision for future amendments. The executive power is vested in a President and Vice President, and the legislative in a Senate and House of Representatives, all chosen by the people.

The same Providence that granted victory to our fathers in the hour of battle, gave them wisdom in a day of peace to devise means of securing to their children the independence they had won. May their prosperity, to the latest generation, daily, look to the Giver of every good and perfect gift for wisdom, that they enjoy the blessing of a free and happy people, whose God is their Lord.

FOUNDING FACTS

This chapter is a short, informational section revealing a few facts about a few of our Founders, including the false one, Thomas Pain(e). These were found in various books written about the Founders, yet none of this appears in current history hooks.

George Washington

The name of George Washington calls up many thrilling emotions in the minds of every American citizen.

He was the third son of Augustine Washington, born February 22, 1732, near the banks of the Potomac, in Westmoreland County, Virginia. His father, in 1730, married, for his second wife, Miss Mary Ball, who bore four sons: George, John, Samuel, and Charles, and one daughter, Betty. His great grandfather, John Washington, emigrated from the north of England about the year 1657 and settled on the place where George was born. At the age of ten, Washington lost his father, and his mother became his sole guardian and instilled into his mind those principles of religion and virtue which formed the solid basis of a character that has been the admiration of statesmen and philosophers wherever the name of the American republic is known. It was the teachings of his sainted mother that prepared his mind for those scenes of strife and turmoil through which he had to pass and that made him a fit instrument *in* the hand of the Heavenly Father. The plan, designed to lift the chains of oppression from the people, guided this child to lead his country over the stormy sea of war into the harbor of peace and liberty. He was remarkable in his strict adherence to truth and for the fond affection, he had for his mother. So much, that when he had received a midshipman's warrant to enter the English navy, her tears had him removing his bags from the ship and determined not to go. This was the first decision from the hand of Providence.

Current history books tell us that Washington caught a cold that led to his death, but another medical reason was the actual cause.

His breathing became laborious, yet he bore all with Christian resignation.

"I die hard," said he, "but I am not afraid to die. I believed, from the first, that I will not survive it. My breath can not last long."

Some hours before his death, after repeated efforts to be understood, he succeeded in expressing a desire that he might be permitted to die without interruption.

Our beloved first President actually died after suffering from a series of strokes.

E C McGuire, *1836*, revealed these facts in *The Religious Opinion and Character of Washington*. It was the only reference I have that included this information.

Morally and intellectually, he was a man from his youth up. Can it be that Washington is dead? No.

> The woods are peopled with his fame;
> His memory wraps the dusky mountains,
> His spirit sparkles o'er the fountains;
> The meanest rill, the mightiest river,
> Roll mingling with his name forever![69]

Thomas Jefferson

Thomas Jefferson was born on April 2, 1743, at Shadwell, in Albemarle County, Virginia. Educated at the college of William and Mary, in Williamsburg, receiving his law degree at twenty-one, he was admitted to the bar and in the following year was chosen as a representative to the provincial legislature. From early youth his mind was imbued with liberal political sentiments. On one of his seals, he had engraved, "Resistance to tyrants in obedience to God."

On June 21, 1775, he took a seat in the general Congress and was appointed, with Adams, to draft the Declaration of Independence, which was adopted July 4, 1776. He held the governorship of Virginia, as a delegate to Congress from Virginia, secretary of state, and vice president, and from March 4, 1801 to 1809, he was president of the United States.[70]

Separation of Church and State is a phrase we live with every day and was determined, by *a few,* to mean Jefferson wanted government and church completely separated. These few have imposed that all reference to religion must be removed from government buildings, schools, and public squares. These few have imposed false meaning of these words on the American people.

The Church of England imposed taxes on every person in Virginia, whether they were members or of a Protestant faith. Every person paid to support the church. Jefferson, as governor, changed this church policy by decree and thus freed the people of Virginia of paying to support the established Church of England. When Virginia declared statehood, the citizens were afraid the Massachusetts Catholics, who were still tied to the Church of England, would settle in their state, get elected to office, and make them change their declared religion (Protestant). They wrote of this in their Constitution, and to this day their words still appear in the Tennessee Constitution, the past territory of Virginia, which reads as follows:

> Article IX-Disqualifications—Section I. Whereas ministers of the Gospel are by their profession, dedicated to God and the care of souls, and ought not be diverted from the great duties of their functions; therefore, no minister of the Gospel, or priest of any denomination whatever, shall not be eligible to a seat in either House of the Legislature.
>
> Section 2. No person who denies the being of God, or future state of rewards and punishments, shall hold any office in the civil department of this state![71]

This they felt would forever protect their right to worship freely.

The Danbury Baptist Association (their ministers were the judges rending judicial proceedings) was chastised when President Jefferson wrote them a letter telling the judges to stop using the Baptist Constitution on the bench and only use the Federal Constitution when rendering judicial decisions. They wrote back, saying, "They would erect a wall, as in Jerusalem, and *separate* their *Church* doctrine from the *State* [Federal] Constitution when rending decisions from the bench" (Author's emphasis). In plain words, he was thumping judges for imposing their ideology from the bench as representatives of the federal government and not following the law of the United States of America![72]

Little is written why the Danbury Baptist Association was using the church's doctrine instead of the Federal Constitution to render judicial decisions. In 1793, an event known as the "X,Y & Z Incident" occurred, and we almost went to war with France (they wanted to conquer England and tried to force us to help them). Some of the different church branches saw an opportunity to try and impose an established church on America. Of course, each thought their doctrines were the chosen of God and everyone should convert to their way. Jefferson had his hands full, and the radicals attacked him in various publications, calling him an atheist, a deist, and some forged letters turned up in France. There were even attacks on George Washington's character. The main publisher was Benjamin Bache. Some *of* the instigators were Joel Barlow, Thomas Paine, and various French officials, one being Genet. They, all tried to start a war, with promises of wealth and positions. Jefferson did not sway in his belief of freedom *of* religion, and finally, by 1801 in a letter to Moses Robinson, he wrote:

> I know, indeed, that there are some of their leaders who have so committed themselves that pride, if no other passion, will prevent their coalescing. We must be easy with them. The eastern States will be the last to come over on account of the dominion of the clergy, who had got a smell of union between Church and State, and begun to indulge reveries, which can never be realized in the present state of science. But I

am in hopes their good sense will dictate them, that since the mountain will not come to them, they had better go to the mountain: that they will find their interest in acquiescing in the liberty and science of their country, and that the Christian religion, when divested of the rags in which they have enveloped it, and brought to the original purity and simplicity of its benevolent institutor, is a religion of all others most friendly to liberty, science, and the freest expression of the human mind.

I sincerely wish with you, we could see our government so secured as to depend on the character of the person in whose hands it is trusted. Bad men will sometimes get in, and, with such an immense patronage, may make great progress in corrupting the public mind and principals. This is a subject with which wisdom and patriotism should be occupied.

I pray you to accept assurances of my high respect and esteem.

Th: Jefferson[73]

Jefferson died on July 4, 1826, at the age of eighty-three, quietly, without murmur or a groan.

A little juicy information: Jefferson loved to partake of the ladies, all ages, colors, and class. When he became President, one of the bishops at his church took him aside and told him to stop this foolishness. The President cannot be doing this, he said. The bishop of the church was Bishop Clinton.

Thomas Pain(e)

I recently purchased a book called *46 Pages*, by Scott Liell. It is a book telling about how Thomas Pain(e) was a Founding Father. The lies throughout this book, giving this scalywag the same status as our true Founders, made me write this dispute.

The only thing I will give Pain(e) (and yes, his name was actually spelled Pain; the T Paine found on so many founding documents belonged to Robert Treat Paine, a true patriot for the cause) is that he did write an inflaming pamphlet entitled "Common Sense." His hatred for England is a story in itself. This pamphlet, along with countless others, demanded freedom from a tyrannical king and a domineering empire. Pain was commissioned by Congress to be the Commissioner of Foreign Affairs. He had access to all the correspondence, including intelligence from different foreign countries. It was discovered that he was in conspiracy with Silas Deane to discredit General George Washington and Dr. Benjamin Franklin to which he was allowed to resign.[74]

Pain was not a founding father.

I will tell you he was a con artist, thief, scalywag, and liar. His first wife, with a child, "disappeared" on a trip with Pain, and he claimed she died having the baby. His second wife, after being beaten and abused, paid him off to get rid of him; he cheated countless people in his scams and was a devout atheist, which some of his later writings attest to and almost got him tarred and feathered. He fled to France (had left England earlier because of warrants against him) and was a party to the revolution and uprising that left that country destroyed.

"A life that is one continued scene"

"Of all, that's infamous and mean"[75]

SOME INTERESTING FACTS AND WORD MEANINGS

These are a few words I picked out because of the present happenings in the world.

Words or phrases have a tendency to change meanings, depending on who embraces and uses them. Several words that, today, receive negative responses actually once had positive meanings. Some started out as describing words, then became negative, and now have a positive reaction. I have chosen three words from today's vocabulary that have a surprising history.

Baghdad

Today, this is the name of the town in Iraq that is embroiled in turmoil and war.

Dad was a Christian Monk. He settled on the banks of the Euphrates River, in the Babylonia fertile valley, the triangle between the rivers of Assyria, known as the Plains of Al-Ja-Zira. He built his cell. Dad was an avid gardener, and to irrigate his gardens he built underground tunnels from the river. When the Persian King Selucia saw his beautiful gardens, he decided to build a city.

Bagh is Persian for a garden. The *Gardens of Dad*-Baghdad is named after a Christian Monk.[76]

Yankee

You may wish to know the origin of the word Yankee. It was a cant, favorite word with farmer Jonathan Hastings of Cambridge, about 1713

Two aged ministers from the college in that town have stated they remember the word to have been in use among the students, but they had no recollection of it before that period.

The inventor used it to express excellence. A Yankee good horse and excellent cider are some examples. The students used to hire horses from him. His use of the term led them to adopt it, and they gave him the name of Yankee Jon. He was a worthy, honest man, but no genius.

Yankee probably became a byword to express a weak, simple, awkward person, and it was carried by them from the college and circulated throughout the country. It was respectful till it was taken up and applied to the New Englanders in common as a term of reproach.

Northerners were called Yankees in the Civil War. Other countries call all Americans Yankees, and we dubbed one of our favorite baseball teams the Yankees.[77]

Niggar

Pronounced nee-gar, Niger comes from the Greek word Niyep, meaning *black*. Today this word has a negative response, causing hurt and embarrassment.

When the Dutch sailed into the bay of Jamestown (1619) they had a cargo. The colonists who lived there were unknowingly being used to rid the Dutch ship of this cargo. Nineteen ebony-skinned males had been sold to the Dutch of Negroland (Africa). The tribe was conquered and the males sold into slavery. The Neegars had been a prosperous group whose ancestors had settled in the Nigger valley for centuries. The colonists did not want captives but willing servants. The Dutch captain threatened to drown them, and life here was better than in their native land so the colonists let them stay.[78]

After the ship had sailed, the Neegars were settled as Negro servants, and they joined the colony. A descendant was William Lee, G. Washington's personal manservant and director of his plantation.[79] He followed our First President into the Revolution. He was injured in a wagon accident, paralyzed from the waist down. Another one of the servants made him a chair with wheels, and William continued to run the plantation from his "wheeled chair." He was given his freedom (freedom was granted to all the servants) in G. Washington's will. William was bequeathed living expenses for the rest of his life. Washington requested, if possible if all would remain on the plantation (leaving could have gotten them in bondage again, as it was the law). They all remained, by their choice, and ran the plantation.

Have you ever wondered why black preachers in this country have such passion in their service to God?

Going back even further, the Neegars came out of the Niger valley, and they were the children of the Ethiopian Princess Tharbis of Saba. An Egyptian Prince had conquered her. This Prince was the warrior who acquired land for the Pharaoh and was on a campaign to conquer all of Lower Egypt (Africa). Her beauty conquered him, and he stayed for several years. (It is written when he left he placed on her finger the rings of forgetfulness and memory. This reflects the pagan worship practiced in Egypt)

They had three sons, naming the second Negar. The Egyptian prince was Moses, a Levite, bloodlines of Levi, the only son of Israel, who received no land, only devout service to God, which is passed through the generations.[80]

REFLECTIONS

It is strange that in current history books the first two centuries of this great land's history have been "revised" and in most cases totally changed or completely left out. Biographical sketches of the people who constructed, fought, and loved this country are missing. American youth need to know who these rulers were, their story of public acts, and associate noble thoughts of them. This is a defect that needs to be remedied; for American children, above others, should be taught in connection with the principles of a Republican government. The fact is these patriots were once children in humble life. Under Providence, by their own exertions and virtues, they arose to the highest station in the gift of their country.

The eyes of the world are on America. They are narrowly watching all her operations and scanning her motives for action. From this land of free people, and influence pervades the globe. Much is expected from the American youth, and a deep responsibility rests on our shoulders to make sure they are instructed in the truth. This strange indifference to the study of America's history is manifested throughout our land, and it is time that a better state of things existed. It is surprising how many schools of higher standing entirely exclude it from their classes. Classic Greek and Rome are mastered, histories of England and France not forgotten, but American history is regarded as a simple elementary subject, unworthy of the advanced scholar and, worse, the professor. This is a fact beyond dispute.

I have been questioned how I can state this. The fact is, along with my history books, I have collected school-books, and they prove my claim. From 1788 to 1860, children were taught the origin of this country with pride and patriotism; religion was prevalent and taught in all grades. Colleges had patriotic history lessons. The Founders were treated with reverence and respect. From 1860 to 1880, a new group was entering the education push. Former slaves—most were already educated in reading, writing, and ciphering—needed schools, and many were founded during the late 1800s to early 1900s. I have several of the black college books, and their American history was abundant. One volume was written as one young graduate's thesis called "Colored Girls and Boys Inspiring U.S. History and a Heart to Heart Talk about White Folks," by William Henry Harrison, 1921. The book is filled with historical facts and poetry. It is the only volume I have ever seen.

Books from 1880 to 1940 show a drastic decrease in patriotic reference and an increase in promoting socialism; one even has a swastika on the spine, and it was printed in the United States. The 1940s—1960s saw hundreds of old history books being burned and replaced with the rewritten volumes—same name and author, just most of the history revised or removed. In books from the 1960s to the current day, we see very little about the Revolution, the Founders, and the purpose of the Revolutionary War for freedom. A book called *Roots* tells of a slave and how terrible America was to him. In the book, it states he came here in 1767-America did *not* exist yet and would not for another twenty-one years! This child slave would be thirty-eight years old when America came to be. It happened, but England, not America, brought him here, and in 1770 all the colonies had banned the importation of slaves. During the Revolution, a lot of slaves were killed or carried off by the British. The book caused a terrible divide between American citizens. I just finished reading a Wikipedia entry claiming the Founders were not religious but secular. The scalywag Pain was elevated to the status of Founder. Adams and Congress proclaimed this country was not founded using Christian doctrine when they agreed to the Tripoli Treaty, a treaty of appeasement written by Joel Barlow, a writer (his skills at writing left most snickering) and lawyer who had been, in desperation, hired by Jefferson as agent to Tripoli since Col. Humphrey, commissioner plenipotentiary, was getting tossed out of France since he did not "ask their help" when writing a treaty with the Bey of Algiers (which only cost us $ 114,000 in losses). The new

American aristocrat president, Adams, had just won a vicious political battle against Jefferson for the presidency and was just sworn into office. He was too busy admiring the gushy letters and reveling in his new office, to even read what Barlow had written and had already given to the Bey. If we look at politicians today, most of them sign without ever reading what they just signed. Islamic pirates were holding our ship and citizens, and this got them released. A perfect case of politicians fighting a war from their chairs in Congress and not thinking what the consequences of their lack of information actions would cause. They have learned nothing to this day. These lies are everywhere and are being taught to our children.[81]

This country was founded on Judeo-Christian ethics and beliefs.[82]

There are those who speak as if in despair of the fortunes of our republic. They say political virtue has declined. If so, then the need to infuse patriotism into the breast of the coming generations is mandatory. And what is so likely to affect this national self-preservation, but to give our children the true record of the sublime virtues of Washington and his compatriots, their toils and dangers—their devotion of life and fortune and the sacrifices our liberties have cost.

History is a harp whose strings are swept by the hand of time. It tells the birth of Creation—the uprising of empires—the demise of mighty nations—it sounds in our ears the events that lie scattered along the path of life. Its notes quiver over the graves of greatness and virtue entombed. Its songs are ever varying and will be heard until time severs the strings, as they are emulating the sounds of the world, and history is no more.

This loss only destines man to repeat over and over the consequences that could have been avoided if history had not been lost, changed, or "revised."

HISTORY TEST-GUESS THE YEAR

- America is at war with an empire that wants total control of the world.
- Islamic forces have declared war on America because they do not like her policies.
- Trade is down—spending is up.
- Strong religious influences prevail among the people. The Christian sects are largely increased and exert an important control over public opinion. It becomes aggressive and, with much zeal, attacks the liberals. Religion affects even politics; the liberals are generally Democrats, while the traditionalists are Republican.
- Sounds like 2020? Actually, the year is 1815.[83]

Funny thing about history: it always repeats?

BIBLIOGRAPHY

Gordon's America, 4 Volumes, 1788, By William Gordon
Debates on the Federal Constitution, 4 Volumes, 1827, By Jonathan Elliot
Douglass' America, 2 Volumes, 1760, By William Douglass
British Empire in America, 2 Volumes, 1770, By Mr. Wymne
American Annals, 2 Volumes, 1805, By Abiel Holmes
Annual Register, 1758-1803, 45 Volumes, Edinburgh
History of the Revolution, 2 Volumes, 1822, By Paul Allen
The Religious Opinions & Character of Washington, 1836, By E.C. McGuire
Washington's Letters, 1796, 2 Volumes, By President George Washington
Memoirs Of The Illustrious General G. Washington, by a Citizen, 1809
Life Of Washington, 1814, By David Ramsay
Life Of Washington, 1807, By Aaron Bancroft
Life Of Washington, 1804, 5 Volumes/Atlas, By John Marshall
Olive Branch, By Several Members of the Continental Congress, 1778
Life Of Jefferson, By B.L. Rayner, 1834
Jefferson's Letters, 4 Volumes, 1830, By Thomas Jefferson Randolph
Notes On The State Of Virginia, By Thomas Jefferson, 1801
Porcupine's Works, 12 Volumes, By William Corbbett, 1801
American Military Biography Lives of Officers of the Revolution 1829
Franklin's Works, 2 volumes, 1799, By Benjamin Franklin
A Defense Of The Constitution Of The Government Of The United States, 1797, 3 Volumes, By John Adams

Constitutional Republicanism, 1803, By Benjamin Austin
Robertson's America, 3 Volumes, 1788, By Robert Robertson
History Of Virginia, By Howe, 1845
History Of New Jersey, By Barber/Howe, 1848
History Of Massachusetts, 2 Volumes, Thomas Hutchinson, 1795
History Of Maine, William Williamson, 1832
History of Rhode Island, Samuel G Arnold 1878
History Of Pennsylvania, a Volumes, By Robert Proud, 1788
History Of Vermont, 2 volumes, Samuel Williams' 1809
History Of New Hampshire, Edwin Charleston, 1857
History Of New York, 1831, F. S. Eastman
History Of the Revolution of South Carolina, David Ramsay, 1785
History of South Carolina, David Ramsay, 1809
History Of North Carolina, Hugh Williamson, 1812
History Of Connecticut, Benjamin Trumbull, 1818
History Of Georgia, By R. Howe, 1837
History Of Maryland, James McSherry 1849
William Gouge Hebrewes, 1654
History of the Old Testament, 5 volumes, 1716, Humphrey Prideaux
History of The World, Sir Walter Relegh, 1652
Moses & Aaron, 1648

ENDNOTES

1. William Douglass, *Douglass' America*, 1760, p. 543-566. Mr. Wynne, *British Empire in America*, 1770, p. 516-552 & 1-46.
2. Aaron Bancroft, *Life of Washington*, 1807, p. 1-20, Sidney Press.
3. Henry Howe, *History of Virginia*, 1845, p. 96-105.
4. S.C. Goodrich, *A Pictorial History of America*, 1848, p. 499-501.
5. *Annual Register*, 1765, p. 241, Stamp Act on the American Colonies.
6. Benjamin Franklin in Charles Ramsay's *History of the Revolution*, 1793, p. 58. William Gordon, *Gordon's America*, 1788, p. 127, 1st American Edition, NY.
7. David Ramsay, *History of the American Revolution*, 1793, p. 59-60.
8. S.C. Goodrich, *Pictorial History of America*, 1844, p. 518.
9. S.C. Goodrich, *Pictorial History of America*, 1844, p. 515.
10. John Warner Barber, *History of Massachusetts*, 1839, P. 30-34. William Gordon, *Gordon's America*, 1788, NY, p. 129.
11. *Annual Register*, 1766, p. 46 & 114. Abiel Holmes, *American Annals*, 1805, p. 277.
12. William Gordon, *Gordon's America*, 1788, p. 150-152. *Annual Register*, 1766, p. 71. Abiel Holmes, *American Annals*, 1805, p. 277.
13. Abiel Holmes, *American Annals*, 1805, p. 284-285.
14. David Ramsay, *American Revolution*, 1793, p. 76-85. *Letters of A Pennsylvania Farmer*, 1767, Mr. Dickinson.
15. William Gordon, *Gordon's America*, 1788, NY, p. 196.

16 William Gordon, *Gordon's America,* 1788, p. 240-241.
17 Paul Allan, *American Revolution,* 1822, p. 240-255. Charles Botta, Ottis's Botta, 1821, p. 264-271. William Gordon, *Gordon's America,* 1788, NY, p. 200-205.
18 William Gordon, *Cordon's American War,* 1788, p. 234-236. David Ramsay, *History of the American Revolution,* 1793, p. 100-101.
19 Abiel Holmes, *American Annal,* 1805, p. 307-312.
20 William Gordon, *Gordon's America,* 1788, NY, P. 274-275
21 Paul, Allan, *History of the Revolution,* 1822, p. 180-181.
22 Paul Allan, *History of the Revolution,* 1822, p. 240-241.
23 William Gordon, *Gordon's America,* 1788, NY, p. 322-324
24 Paul Allan, *History of the American Revolution,* 1822, p. 240-247.
25 Paul Allan, *History of American Revolution,* 1822, p. 247-248. American Biography, 1829, Major-General Putnam, p. 255-256.
26 Samuel Williams, *History of Vermont,* 1809, p. 100-108.
27 Abiel Holmes, *American Annal,* 1805, p. 328-330.
28 William Gordon, *Gordon's America, 1788,* p. 251-258.
29 William Gordon, *Gordon's America,* 1788, p. 372-376.
30 Paul Allan, *History of American Revolution,* 1822, p. 325.
31 George Washington, Washington's Letters, 1796, *p.* 8. Aaron Bancroft, *An Essay on the Life of Washington,* 1807, p. 40-41.
32 Paul Allan, *American Revolution,* 1822, p. 322.
33 Paul Allan, *American Revolution,* 1822, p. 306. Charles Botta, *History of the Revolution,* 1821 p. 281-283.
34 Paul Allan, *American Revolution,* 1822, p. 308-311.
35 David Ramsay, *History of the Revolution of South Carolina,* 1785, p. 268-277.
36 America Military Biography, Major-General William Moultrie, 1829, p. 238-242.
37 Charles Botta, *History of the War,* 1821, p. 337-340. Paul Allan, *American Revolution,* 1822, p. 72-77.
38 David Ramsay, *History of South Carolina,* 1809, p. 275.

39 William Gordon, Gordon's America, 1788, p. 289-295. "...and for this declaration, and with firm reliance on the protection of *divine providence*, we mutually pledge to each other our lives, our fortunes and our sacred honor." Declaration of Independence, July 4, 1776. T Jefferson Randolph, *Jefferson's Letters*, 1830, Handwritten draft, Declaration of Independence.

40 Charles Fredrick, *History of the U.S.*, 1825, p. 174-177.

41 Sanderson & Pomeroy, American Biographies, 1823, *History of the Sigers of the Declaration of Independence*, 9 volumes.

42 Paul Allan, *American Revolution*, 1822, p. 401-402.

43 Charles Botta, *History of the Revolution*, 1821, p. 162-164.

44 Charles Goodrich, *History of America*, 1834, 181-182.

45 Aaron Bancroft, *Life of Washington*, 1807, p. 127-130. William Gordon, *Gordon's America*, 1788, p. 393-396.

46 Paul Allan, *American Revolution*, 1822, p. 41-43.

47 William Gordon, *Gordon's American War*, 1788, p. 414-417.

48 M.L. Weems, *Memoirs of La Fayette*, ISIS, p. 53-55. Benjamin Franklin, *Life of Franklin*, 1818, p. 242-252.

49 S.C. Goodrich, *Pictorial History of America*, 1848, p. 595-596.

50 Paul Allan, *American Revolution*, 1822, p. 84.

51 Paul Allan, *American Revolution*, 1822, p. 390-391.

52 Life of La Fayette, *American Military Biographies*, 1829, p. 441.

53 Paul Allan, *American Revolution*, 1822, p. 172-174. William Gordon, *Gordon's American War*, 1788, p. 54-60.

54 Paul Allan, *American Revolution*, 1822, p. 179.

55 Aaron Bancroft, *Life of Washington*, 1807, p. 198-200. American Military Biography, General Charles Lee, 1829, p. 198.

56 American Military Biography, General Charles Lee, 1829, p. 207.

57 F.S. Eastman, *History of New York* 1831 p. 257-262. William Gordon, *Gordon's American Wear*, 1788, p. 207.

58 Abiel Holmes, *American Annals*, 1805, p. 408-409

59 William Gordon, *Gordon's America*, 1788, p. 414-416.

60 Thomas Wilson Biography of Military & Naval Heroes, Israel Putnam, 1819, p. 39. S.C. Goodrich, *Pictorial History of America*, 1848, p. 621-622.

61 S.C. Goodrich, *Pictorial History of America*, 1848, p. 623-625. American Military Biography, Major-General Anthony Wayne, 1829, p. 342-355.

62 American Military Biography, Commodore John Paul Jones, 1829, p. 370-401.

63 Aaron Bancroft, *Life of Washington*, 1807, p. 214-221.

64 American Military Biography, Major-General Francis Marion, 1829, p. 209-215.

65 American Military Biography, the Traitor, Benedict Arnold, 1829, p. 359-365. Aaron Bancroft, *Life of Washington, 1807, p.* 253-261. John Barber & Henry Howe, *History of New Jersey*, 1844, p. 77-78.

66 David Ramsay, *History of the Revolution*, 1795, p. 273-274 William Gordon, *Gordon's America*, 1788, p. 260-262.

67 William Gordon, *Gordon's America*, 1788, p. 380.

68 William Gordon, *Gordon's America*, 1788, p. 401-412, The Constitution of the United States.

69 Aaron Bancroft, *Life of Washington*, 1807, p. 214-221.

70 Henry Howe, *History of Virginia*, 1845, p. 144-145.

71 History of Tennessee, 1886, p. 642-645. Tennessee Constitution 2007.

72 Thomas Jefferson, Notes on Virginia, 1801, p. 235. Henry Howe, *History of Virginia*, 1845, p. 142-145. T Jefferson Randolph, Jefferson's Letters, 1830, 4 volumes.

73 T Jefferson Randolph, Jefferson's Letters, 1830, volume 3, p. 463. Benjamin Bache, Aurora, American Register, 1780-1805. William Cobbett, Porcupine Works, 1801., 12 volumes.

74 William Cobbett, Life of Thomas Pain by Mr. Odeys, Porcupine Works, 1801, p. 73-94 William Gordon, *Gordon's American*, 1788, p. 38-40 & p. 216-222.

75 William Cobbett, Life of Thomas Pain by Mr. Odeys, Porcupine Works, 1801, p. 65. Abiel Holmes, *American Annals*, 1805, p. 353. Paul Allan, *American Revolution*, 1822, p. 346-347.

76 Humphrey Prideaux, *History of the Old Testament*, 1718, p. 572.

77 William Gordon, *Gordon's American War*, 1788, p. 324.

78 John Barber, *History of New Jersey*, 1844, p. 38.

79 Aaron Bancroft, *Life of Washington*, 1807, copy of Washington's Will, p. 533-558.

80 *Moses & Aaron*, 1648, p. 156. Sir Walter Ralegh, *History of the World*, 1652, p. 210. Lewis Ellis, Universal Library of Historians, 1709, p. 42-48. John Payne, *Universal History*, 1793, p. 358-368. *Citizen of Massachusetts, History of US.*, 1821, p. 25.

81 *Laws & Treaties of the United States*, 1796, the sidebar explanation that is not mentioned when claims the Founders wanted America secular without religion reads as follows: *"Pretexts arising from religious opinions not to interrupt the harmony of the two nations" @ America would not cheat them because they were Musslemen and expected the same from them because she was Christian."*

82 Jonathan Elliot Debates on the Federal Constitution-The Declaration of Each Colony to be a Christian State, 1827, p. 485, 20th Amendment. William Gordon, *Gordon's American*, 1788, p.409-417. An Extract from the Act for establishing Religious Freedom passed in the Assembly of Virginia in 1786, p. 419-421.

83 Robert J Bedford, Chronological Order, *History of America*, 1886, p. 119.

www.ingramcontent.com/pod-product-compliance
Ingram Content Group UK Ltd.
Pitfield, Milton Keynes, MK11 3LW, UK
UKHW022224230426
12048UKWH00016BA/1046